BOB DEUTSCH

The Real Estate Agent's *Action Guide* to

LISTING & SALES SUCCESS

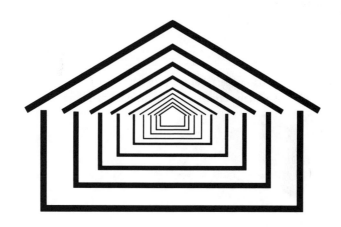

**Real Estate
Education Company**
® a division of Dearborn Financial Publishing, Inc.

While a great deal of care has been taken to provide accurate and current information, the ideas, suggestions, general principles and conclusions presented in this text are subject to local, state and federal laws and regulations, court cases and any revisions of same. The reader is thus urged to consult legal counsel regarding any points of law—this publication should not be used as a substitute for competent legal advice.

Publisher: Kathleen A. Welton
Acquisitions Editor: Patrick J. Hogan
Associate Editor: Karen A. Christensen
Senior Project Editor: Jack L. Kiburz
Interior Design: Lucy Jenkins
Cover Design: David Corona Design

Published by Real Estate Education Company,
a division of Dearborn Financial Publishing, Inc.

Printed in the United States of America.

98 10 9 8 7 6 5 4

Library of Congress Cataloging-in-Publication Data

Deutsch, Bob.
    The real estate agent's action guide to listing and sales success
/ by Bob Deutsch.
        p.   cm.
    Includes index.
    ISBN 0–79310–714–8
    1. Real estate business.   2. Real estate agents.   3. Real estate
agents—Finance, Personal.   I. Title.
HD1375.D48   1993   93-24922
333.33′068′8—dc20   CIP

DEDICATION

To my dad, who taught me determination

To my mom, who taught me responsibility

To my brothers, who taught me competitiveness

To my sister, who taught me to maintain a sense of humor

To my wife, Sheila, who taught me to love and

To my children, Mark, Michael and Michelle, who gave me the reason

Contents

Preface

Welcome to the wonderful world of real estate! You're entering an exciting, highly rewarding, sometimes frustrating business. You will be entrusted with your clients' savings and depended on for the most expert advice. You will become an amateur psychologist, marriage counselor and friend to your clients.

Salespeople in other fields are not as fortunate. They often must educate their prospects to the advantages of investing in their particular commodity in order to continue the sales presentation. In real estate sales, you'll unleash basic motivations: to be free of landlords, to be free to improve their land, to become a homeowner and to fulfill the American dream.

Competency in serving the needs of your clients must be the individual responsibility of each salesperson. You can and must develop yourself fully and thoroughly in your job. Some companies help through orientation and training, but the basic responsibility remains with the individual.

Individuals must also supply *integrity*. Real estate is essentially a collection of individuals; in any one place, at any one time, the integrity of the whole is no greater than that of the individual representing it.

You will experience a great deal of rejection in this business, but no other profession can offer you the personal and financial rewards. Once you experience a successful transaction for a client, you feel elated, motivated and compensated for every rejection or failure that occurred before.

Real estate is the highest-paid hard work or the lowest-paid easy work. Your *motivation* is the key to your success. Will you have motivation or just desire?

Remember . . . If it is to be, it is up to me.

Do you know what motivates you? Do you know what motivates the people around you? The following story is a helpful reminder:

Pete was a good old fellow who decided to become a woodcutter. He was very excited about his new job, and when he started, he could chop wood as well as most anyone. He had a lot of enthusiasm, and it seemed that, cord after cord, the wood piled up. Pete's production was good, and Pete was very happy because he was so pleased with his work.

A strange thing happened to Pete, though. After a while, it seemed that the harder he worked, the less he got done. The wood wasn't piling up like it used to. His production fell and at the same time his frustration grew. Pete wasn't proud of his work anymore and became unhappy. Others in the crew noticed that Pete wasn't as much fun to work with. Finally, one day he threw down his axe in disgust and quit.

Other woodcutters on his crew couldn't understand what had happened to good old Pete. In the beginning, his attitude had been really good. He knew how to produce and was fun to work with. But he had changed. Everyone on the crew had noticed the change. As the others were talking, one of the woodcutters picked up Pete's axe and examined it. He suddenly shouted, "I know why Pete got so angry and quit. His production fell because he was so busy chopping wood, he forgot to sharpen his axe."

Don't be so busy at the woodpile that you forget to sharpen your axe.

The chapters that follow are designed to help you get started, instruct you in each skill, help you develop and give you insight into sales skills and techniques. It cannot be overemphasized that you need to perform all the skills, not just the activities you like. All activities have to be performed consistently for you to be successful. This book has been designed for and is dedicated to keeping your axe sharp.

Remember, stagnation and fermentation improve wine, not the mind.

ABOUT ACTION RECALLS

Throughout the text, in almost every chapter, are ACTION recalls. The sole purpose of the ACTION recalls is to jog your memory. These ACTION recalls should be reviewed in sales meetings and in one-to-one meetings with your manager. However, proceed with caution. Do not try to review more than three ACTION recalls at any one time. The opportunity for internalization must not be defeated due to the burden of too much, too soon.

Keep frustration at a minimum, and maintain your motivation. Accelerated motivation will occur with the swelling of self-confidence. Success will come sooner, and your success will be for an unlimited duration. Participate whole-heartedly in this most exciting of all sports—that of living your life.

Good Luck. . .
—Bob Deutsch

Skills for Listing and Selling Real Estate

The practice of real estate is at once focused and broadbased, requiring a mastery of a wide range of skills. For your convenience I have listed these skills below based on where they appear in this book.

Chapter 1

- Plan professional growth
- Analyze communication
- Understand the steps in estate planning
- Analyze your motivations and desires thoroughly and honestly

Chapter 2

- Set objectives that work

Chapter 3

- Develop a competitive market analysis

Chapter 4

- Take charge over the telephone
- Get the appointment over the telephone
- Overcome ad and sign call objections
- Have a good reason when prospect telephoning
- Overcome prospect objections over the telephone
- Pinpoint areas for growth in telephone technique

Chapter 5

- Work with walk-ins confidently
- Use spare time creatively

Chapter 6

- Qualify buyers
- Balance your time between "ready" and "money" time
- Manage your listing bank
- Create a neighborhood directory
- Prospect creatively
- Contacting FSBOs confidently
- Have door-to-door prospecting know-how
- Approach an expired listing
- Develop a prospecting plan
- List the property
- Build an effective mailing list
- Organize an ongoing direct mail campaign

Chapter 7

- Develop and monitor a plan for servicing the listing
- Develop and monitor a plan for the listing package

Chapter 8

- Conduct a professional open house
- Use the 12 basics of effective ads

Chapter 9

- Use vivid home descriptions in classified ads
- Write headlines and ad copy that control action

Chapter 10

- Structure a client contact so that it becomes a sale
- Make the buying decision the most natural thing in the world
- Handle objections in the decision-making stage
- Prepare yourself for showing property
- Prepare the seller for showing property
- Prepare the buyer for showing property
- Handle objections in showing property
- Show property to its best advantage
- Get the buyer to make an offer
- Write the offer with professional precision
- Present the offer
- Represent the buyer and the seller

Chapter 11

- Earn the loyalty of past clients
- Earn the business of corporate clients
- Rise above both depression and success

1 The Development of Me

This book focuses on your job: getting started, working the service area, making the sale and maintaining the proper attitude throughout.

Let's take the last item mentioned above, proper attitude, and explore it further for a moment.

Later in this book, you'll get an idea of what viewpoint you can best use to successfully perform any job-related skill. You'll be asked to view each skill from a positive point of view; how you view a skill or technique will determine how well you perform. If you see it in the proper light, you will make it work for you.

There is very little difference in people, but that difference makes a big difference. The difference is attitude: Is it negative or positive?

Nowhere is this principle better illustrated than in the story of the young bride following her husband to an Army camp on the edge of the California desert. Living conditions were primitive at best. Her husband advised against it, but she wanted to be with him. The only housing they could find was a rundown shack near an Indian village. The heat was unbearable in the daytime—115 degrees in the shade. The wind blew constantly, spreading dust and sand all over. The days were long and boring. Her only neighbors were Indians, none of whom spoke English. When her husband was ordered further into the desert for two weeks of maneuvers, loneliness and the wretched living conditions began to take their toll. She wrote to her mother informing her she was coming home. She just couldn't endure any more. In a few days she received a reply from her mother. It had these two lines:

> Two men looked out from prison bars,
> One saw mud, the other saw stars.

She read the lines over and over and began to feel ashamed of herself. She didn't really want to leave her husband. All right, she'd look for the stars. In the following days, she set out to make friends with the Indians. She asked them to teach her weaving and pottery. At first they were distant, but as soon as they sensed her interest was genuine, they returned her friendship. She became fascinated with their culture, history, with everything about them. She began to study the desert as well, and soon it changed from a desolate, forbidding place to a marvelous thing of beauty. She had her mother send her books. She began to study the cacti, the yucca plants, the Joshua trees. She collected seashells that had been left millions of years ago, when the sands had been an ocean floor. Later, she became such an expert on the area that she wrote a book about it.

What had changed? Not the desert; not the Indians. By changing her attitude, she had transformed a miserable experience into a highly rewarding one.

What is self-development? Why bring it up? Self-development is a never-ending cycle. Any increasing awareness and knowledge you obtain about yourself, your interests and the way you affect others will manifest itself in your life, attitude and work performance.

You are what you want to be. In this section, we will give you some ideas about what self-development is and can be. After all, we are referring to *your* personal growth; what you do about it is your decision.

Remember . . . If it is to be, it is up to me.

Instructive Options

The major contributor to your growth is knowledge—knowledge and understanding of yourself, your special interests, your job, your job-related interests, other people and a multitude more. You can pursue your new knowledge through several avenues, based on your own preferences:

Conferences
- Sales meetings (in your office)
- Special training sessions (in your office)
- Regional meetings and training seminars

Seminars Offered Outside
- Specialized real estate–oriented seminars, advertised through local media and the local Board of REALTORS®
- Guest speakers (offered by the Board)
- Special-interest seminars, sessions offered covering a topic of interest to you, advertised in local media

Local College Courses
- Regular classes, covering a multitude of subjects, from real estate skills to topics of a more personal nature
- One-day seminars covering specific subjects
- Workshops covering many different subjects

Books, Audiotapes and Videotapes
- Real estate skills and concepts
- Special interests and subjects (consult bookstores or libraries for information)

Membership in Professional Associations
- Magazines and books that help keep you aware of current events and trends in your business
- Attendance at seminars or workshops that enable you to exchange professional information with other real estate salespeople

The more knowledge you seek, no matter what form it takes, the more satisfying your professional sales life will be.

How Many Cylinders Am I Working On?   The following checklist is designed to assist you in evaluating your sales performance. You can also use this checklist to guide your development in the early months of your sales career.

Salespeople often ask, "What do I need to know to reach my goals?", "What am I not doing that I should be doing?" and "How will I know when I am working toward proper goals?" To answer these questions accurately, review the following material, but only when you can give it your *complete attention*. Be absolutely honest—you should become the best evaluator of yourself and your business.

Discuss your self-evaluation with your sales manager and ask for advice or assistance. Following the self-evaluation section, we offer some tips on self-improvement, responding to some commonly asked questions.

PERFORMANCE CHECKLIST

Check "yes" or "no" for each answer.

I. Developing Clientele

Yes	No		
☐	☐	1.	I have studied the market potential within my sales area. I know how to find prospective buyers and owners who can give me the sales production I want.
☐	☐	2.	I make use of as many main avenues of prospecting as I can each week, and systematically plan my activity in this area day by day.
☐	☐	3.	I ask for referred leads, even if the contact did not result in business. I have, and use, a good referred lead talk.
☐	☐	4.	I have attempted to prospect within situations having long-range potential during the past month.
☐	☐	5.	I make use of a daily record system of keeping mailing lists, prospect files, ownership change files and so forth. I maintain such information as unfulfilled needs, rather than just names and addresses.
☐	☐	6.	At least once every two months, I call on prospective clients in my own listing bank or farm area for potential business so as to develop new business or referred leads.
☐	☐	7.	I use my powers of personal observation by scanning newspapers, For Sale signs and so forth for new listings or prospective buyers.

Yes   **No**

❏   ❏   8. I recognize "shoppers" before I waste a tremendous amount of time and energy on them.

❏   ❏   9. I have attempted to upgrade my market prospects and the size of an average deal within the last year.

❏   ❏   10. I have a full understanding of the importance of prospecting.

Score: Add all "no" answers, multiply by 10 and deduct from 100%. If you have a "no," do you have a plan to make it a "yes"?

II. Sales Skills

Yes   **No**

❏   ❏   1. I learn as much as I can about prospective buyers and sellers before I call on them.

❏   ❏   2. I start each interview by discussing something I know will interest the customer, such as a compliment or an offer of service.

❏   ❏   3. I am enthusiastically aggressive; I strive to make each succeeding meeting or presentation better than the last.

❏   ❏   4. I look and act confident; I always appear to be relaxed rather than tense or anxious, when I'm with a prospective buyer or seller.

❏   ❏   5. I am confident of my material and have a good command of the facts.

❏   ❏   6. I put myself in the customer's shoes, determining his or her primary needs and tailoring my sales methods accordingly.

❏   ❏   7. I know how to address objections skillfully.

❏   ❏   8. I ask questions and use feedback to make sure the customer understands and appreciates the benefits and opportunities I offer.

❏   ❏   9. I sell through the eye as well as the ear and make full use of visual displays whenever I can.

❏   ❏   10. I always ask the prospective buyer or seller to take action. I emphasize benefits and explain their significance to him or her when I close; I close as many times as is practical.

Score: Add all "no" answers, multiply by 10 and deduct from 100%. If you have a "no," do you have a plan to make it a "yes"?

III. Market Knowledge and Skillful Growth

Yes   **No**

☐   ☐   1. I know my company's entire range of services and use them effectively.

☐   ☐   2. I am actively involved in a formal continuing education program.

☐   ☐   3. During the past year, I have taken self-improvement courses in sales skills, public speaking or creative thinking. I have also read more than one book on sales techniques in the past year.

☐   ☐   4. I diligently seek out and study worthwhile sales material to help me grow on a professional basis. I apply it to my work.

☐   ☐   5. I contribute to the group and gain as much as I can during office sales meetings.

☐   ☐   6. I belong to an outside organization within my community. I regularly attend meetings and other events.

☐   ☐   7. I keep well informed and well read on national and local influences that affect my business, such as changes in zoning matters, population changes and marketing trends.

☐   ☐   8. I have a positive attitude and avoid "knocking the competition" from other brokers.

☐   ☐   9. I have a full understanding of the ethical nuances of my business and scrupulously avoid violating good ethical practice.

☐   ☐   10. I am proud to be associated with this company and feel that I provide it and its clients a valuable service.

Score: Add all "no" answers, multiply by 10 and deduct from 100%. If you have a "no," do you have a plan to make it a "yes"?

IV. Work Habits

Yes   **No**

☐   ☐   1. I plan my work each day in advance so I know exactly what I intend to do and what I want to accomplish.

☐   ☐   2. I ask myself regularly, "What are the most important things I must do?" I set priorities and follow through.

☐   ☐   3. I work longer hours and make more sales calls than most salespeople.

Yes   **No**

❏   ❏   4. I organize my time in the office to do those things that should be done, such as a predetermined number of telephone calls and mailings each day.

❏   ❏   5. I set aside and use time each day for prospecting, interviewing, delivering documents and so on.

❏   ❏   6. I try to increase my success by reviewing my previous week's work efforts and by planning a systematic self-improvement program to improve performance in the coming week.

❏   ❏   7. I periodically analyze my own reactions and try to understand myself so I can maintain a positive mental attitude and emotional state.

❏   ❏   8. I face and solve problems instead of ignoring them and allowing them to become insurmountable.

❏   ❏   9. I constantly strive to improve my prospecting techniques and selling skills.

❏   ❏   10. I refuse to feel sorry for myself when I have a bad day. I analyze each meeting I had to determine how it could be improved.

Score: Add all "no" answers, multiply by 10 and deduct from 100%. If you have a "no," do you have a plan to make it a "yes"?

V. Am I a People Person?

Yes   **No**

❏   ❏   1. Prospects and clients consider me an authority in my field.

❏   ❏   2. I remember birthdays, anniversaries and other important occasions, and send a card or note to let my prospects and clients know I remembered.

❏   ❏   3. I am reliable and I keep my promises. I provide service as promised.

❏   ❏   4. I keep my name in front of my best prospects and clients by sending out monthly mailings.

❏   ❏   5. I actively associate with a community service group and try to get on committees that will build my experience and exposure.

❏   ❏   6. I continually work to improve my communication skills.

Yes	No		
❏	❏	7.	I am a good listener. I listen sincerely without interrupting.
❏	❏	8.	I am tactful. I avoid telling people I meet, "You're wrong." I keep my personal opinions to myself so that I can try to understand people better and discover what makes them tick.
❏	❏	9.	When I conclude a deal, I always write thank-you notes and follow up to show my appreciation.
❏	❏	10.	I cooperate with my office colleagues.

Score: Add all "no" answers, multiply by 10 and deduct from 100%. If you have a "no," do you have a plan to make it a "yes"?

VI. Am I Truly a Professional?

Yes	No		
❏	❏	1.	I am always well groomed.
❏	❏	2.	I look and act the part of a valued member of the real estate community.
❏	❏	3.	I speak clearly, enthusiastically and correctly.
❏	❏	4.	I am in good health and I show it.
❏	❏	5.	I have a genuine interest in people and their problems.
❏	❏	6.	I go out of my way to help people and organizations.
❏	❏	7.	I try daily to improve my vocabulary and memory.
❏	❏	8.	I have a good smile and a friendly, positive, cheerful manner.
❏	❏	9.	I try to be myself rather than a pale imitation of someone else.
❏	❏	10.	I have a long-range plan for the economic security of my family. I have discussed it with an estate planning authority and have adopted his or her suggestions.

Score: Add all "no" answers, multiply by 10 and deduct from 100%. If you have a "no," do you have a plan to make it a "yes"?

ACTION BAROMETER

After you complete the preceding checklist, make a dot in each of the following columns, indicating the score you gave yourself for that particular trait. Then draw a line connecting the dots.

The resulting graphic profile will reveal your weaknesses and your strengths. You'll see what needs to be strengthened. You may wish to discuss your profile with your manager.

	100	90	80	70	60	50	40	30	20	10
Developing Clientele										
Sales Skills										
Market Knowledge and Skillful Growth										
Work Habits										
Am I a People Person?										
Am I Truly a Professional?										

100 = Excellent   80 = Good   60 = Fair   40–20 = Poor, Needs Plan To Improve

ACTION COMMITMENTS

I have read the previous section and realize I must do the following:

TO DO	TARGET DATE OF COMPLETION	ACTION COMPLETED
1.		
2.		
3.		
4.		
5.		
6. Meet with sales manager.		

SELF-IMPROVEMENT PLAN

Action Step 1   List your ten greatest limitations. Discuss them with your manager to work out a program to improve one weakness each week for ten weeks.

Action Step 2   Sit down with several other salespeople and develop a list of all the ways to open a prospecting interview; use this list when appropriate.

Action Step 3   Get together with several other salespeople and practice using various closing techniques.

Action Step 4   Prospects are interested in themselves. They like to do business with a salesperson who demonstrates a helpful attitude. Too frequently, salespeople violate this basic concept by overusing the word *I* instead of *you*. For one week, see how many phrases you can switch from the "I" approach.

Action Step 5 List all the probing questions you can think of to find out what a customer truly needs. Discuss the questions with several other sales agents and get additional ideas from them.

Action Step 6 List all the possible objections a customer can bring up for not buying. Evaluate the importance of each objection as a stumbling block in completing a transaction, and analyze the frequency with which the objections occur. Think up as many counters to these objections as you can. Discuss these comebacks with your manager.

Action Step 7 Keep track of how much time you spend in one week on such matters as face-to-face meetings with prospects, auto travel, use of the telephone, records and so on. Analyze how you can use your time more effectively and develop a schedule for the following week.

Action Step 8 Try for one week to pause in the following situations in a sales interview:

- After making an important selling point
- After answering a question or objection
- When you want the prospect to say or think about something

Action Step 9 Read a book on the psychology of selling. Check yourself for one week to determine whether you are saying or doing things that create resistance, such as, "To tell you the truth" or "Everybody is doing this." Also, if you stand or sit too close to a prospective buyer or seller or offend his or her political, moral or social beliefs, you are certain to create trouble for yourself.

Action Step 10 Make certain that your manager understands in detail exactly how you are spending your time, and how this relates to your short-term goals.

Action Step 11 Set up a contest with another salesperson in connection with some activity that you want to improve, such as prospecting or closing.

Action Step 12   Each day, for at least one week, make a point of doing something extra for a prospective buyer or seller—something above and beyond the call of duty.

Action Step 13   Every time you make a first-time sale to a new customer, write him or her a personal thank-you letter.

Action Step 14   Make up your mind today that you are going to make every day a listening day. Listen to everyone as much as possible and talk to each person you contact as little as possible.

Action Step 15   Set down ten target prospects you are going to try to get to do some specific thing, such as list with you or buy. When you have "sold" one, add another prospect to your target list.

WHAT DID I SAY?

Good communication doesn't depend entirely on listening to what the other person has to say. You have to know how to listen to yourself as well.

Selling real estate is a process of communicating to a buyer that a particular property fully satisfies his or her realty needs while staying within his or her economic capabilities. This definition makes a complex merchandising process sound absurdly simple, but selling is not simple, because the key word in the definition is *communication*.

You can't market real estate without communicating. Getting the listing, advertising the property, showing it, selling and closing all involve exchanges of great quantities of information through a variety of media. It all seems so normal that we may not realize the complexity of the process or how we can control the results.

Communication is more than just talking to another person; the physical and mental process of speaking is intricate. When you put together a sentence that sounds good, you feel pleased with the result and forget that the job is only half-done. The job is not complete until the other person understands what you are saying.

Communication occurs only when two people see something in a similar way; the more alike their understanding, the greater the degree of communication.

Five-Part Model

Unfortunately, you cannot control your prospect's ability to communicate, but you can learn to control your own effectiveness as a communicator. How? By understanding each aspect of the communication process. One model breaks the process into five parts:

1. Who is talking?
2. What is said?
3. To whom is the message delivered?
4. Through what medium?
5. With what effect?

Let's examine each aspect in terms of how you can control it.

Who Is Talking?   As a salesperson, you are aware of the importance of any person's credentials. Is it a new salesperson or an established broker? Is it someone with professional designations, a successful track record or an impeccable reputation? A speaker's credentials affect how well you listen when that person talks about real estate. In the same way, your credentials affect how well a prospective buyer or seller listens to you.

Establish your image or credibility as a real estate expert early in the relationship with your customer. There is little opportunity or reason to tell about your credentials over the phone, so get your prospective buyers or sellers into your office or get into their home, and then build your image by references to specifics that show you are knowledgeable, informed and able to fill their needs.

Good grooming and dress, a well-kept desk and office, and evidence of professionalism, organization and a working staff all signify that you are an effective businessperson. Certificates of membership in real estate organizations, sales charts, maps, pamphlets and listing books all help convey your ability to get things done.

At this point, you are preparing the customer to listen to you. One communication expert declares that the success of the communication process depends on the willing receptivity of the listener. Remember: The most beautiful, precisely articulated message is lost if no one is listening.

Don't feel that this image-building creates a false impression. You know you're an expert—let others know it too. If you insist on operating with a low company or personal profile, you must work unnecessarily hard to overcome negative impressions. This labor certainly can be spent in more profitable ways.

What Is Said?   This element of the model covers the realm of semantics. Words are symbols; they represent things, but are not the things themselves. People create different mental pictures of the things words represent. For example, if you ask several people to draw a house in detail, you will get several different pictures, because we all see different typical houses.

What is said also refers to the nonverbal signals we use. These signals are classified in the study of body language. Combinations of individual body movements, or *kines*, symbolize a language more precise than that which is spoken; its interpretation, however, is even more difficult.

Develop a sense of what others say to you through their body language and of what your body language says about you. You can do this partly through reading, but mostly through observation. You should, however, be as cautious in interpreting nonverbal signals as you are with words. Don't jump to conclusions or generalize from one gesture or body movement.

To Whom Is the Message Delivered?   You wouldn't talk to residential buyers about industrial property, office buildings or commercial listings. This selectivity should apply to all communication attempts. You must deliver the message to the right person.

To do this, you must select the decision maker in the transaction. Is it the husband, the wife or the relative with the cash for the down payment? You must pay attention to the non–decision makers, but separate their comments or communications from the important ones. You are trying to match thoughts with a document signer, a difficult process in itself. Don't let the statements of others who are trying to help the discussion cloud the issues.

Once you have selected the decision maker, make certain that person gets the information necessary to make the buying decision. Hear what the listener needs to hear, then provide the information as clearly as possible.

Through What Medium?   The medium must suit the message for *maximum effectiveness*. Should you

- send a letter?
- telephone?
- send a telegram?
- do it in person?

The telephone is fine for setting an appointment with the seller or to show the house, but it is most likely the wrong medium through which to inform the seller of an offer. In every situation, one medium is most appropriate for the message. Using your experience and judgment, you must predict which will work best.

With What Effect?   What finally happens is the test of all communication. "Pass the salt" is good communication, if the salt is passed. "Please approve this" is a perfect close, if the signature is appropriately inked. You must know the goal of each communication attempt. If that goal is not accomplished, you didn't communicate.

To check your progress toward your goal, use techniques for getting feedback:

1. Listen to yourself. Ask yourself, "Have I chosen the best words? Do my sentences make sense and sound clear? Am I using the right amount of volume and energy?" Repeat and rephrase your message until you think it is getting across. Remember that your message is not a neat series of sentences or paragraphs blocked out in your mind, but a series of random images from which you draw.

2. Look at your listener. Observe his or her body language and listen to his or her comments. Is the listener interested? Is a response negative or positive? If negative, change your presentation.

3. Get your listener to verbalize his or her feelings. Again, use open-ended questions. The more your listener talks, the more information you have.

4. Keep in mind the principle of selective perception: All communication attempts involve high levels of selectivity. In many ways, people choose what they will or will not listen to. If a prospect is unhappy with you or if your credibility is in question, he or she will not listen to you. You, in turn, must

select the proper information, the best words and the most effective medium of expression.

People select how much they will remember. Experts estimate that 65 percent is forgotten as soon as it is heard. The balance fades rapidly as the listener's comprehension decreases. The whole process resembles "fugutive art," an ice sculpture that shrinks in the sun, unless specific efforts are made to provide permanence.

So don't be too quick to interpret what is said to you and don't assume that your words have been interpreted correctly. Become supercritical of your language and alert to possible misunderstandings.

The simplest way to make sure you understand what the customer wants is to ask questions. Use open-ended questions that require the listener to think, and to give more than just "yes" and "no" answers. For example, when a buyer says, "I want some land with a house," don't ask "An acre?" The response might be "yes," but has this told you how this person visualizes the size of an acre? A better question would be, "Why do you want the land?" or "How do you plan to use it?" These questions let you get a sense of how the buyer sees "some land."

Avoid playing word games. Just how big is "a nice-sized lot," or how many dollars are involved in "low taxes?" Of course, descriptive words cannot be perfect representations, but don't let semantic camouflage creep into your presentations and make your language so imprecise that nothing is clearly represented.

Unclear communication results in dissatisfied buyers. Leave abstract painting to the artists and look for realism in your work. Spend time discussing buyers' needs, and don't be too quick to jump into your car for a listing tour. Ask for definitions, find specifics and make sure your work pictures match—*then* begin the search. Continually recheck definitions to make sure they haven't changed. Keep talking, keep digging, keep comparing.

For each part of the communication process, evaluate yourself:

- *Who is talking?* Am I speaking from the highest level of credibility possible?
- *What is being said?* Am I choosing my words as carefully as possible?
- *To whom?* Am I directing my message to the right person?

- *In what medium?* Is this the best channel for this message?
- *With what effects?* Is my goal being achieved?

Realizing that good communication requires work can put you on the road to improvement. Why not ask others for their opinions? Record some of your conversations and play them back. You'll soon spot some weaknesses and develop alternatives.

Effective communication techniques can be learned. The results will be your passport to greater satisfaction and personal achievement—if you work at listening to yourself and to others.

ACTION COMMITMENTS

I have read the previous section and realize I must do the following:

TO DO	TARGET DATE OF COMPLETION	ACTION COMPLETED
1.		
2.		
3.		
4.		
5.		
6. Meet with sales manager.		

FINANCIALLY PLAN AHEAD

Overhead on the beach: "Mommy, may I go in for a swim?" "Certainly not, dear, it's far too deep." "But Daddy is swimming." "Yes, dear, but he's insured."

Estate Planning

Let's begin with a definition of *Estate Planning*. The formal definition is "The creation, conservation and utilization of family resources to obtain maximum support and security for the family, during the lifetime and after the death of the planner." More simply stated, it's making the most of what you have or can develop.

It sounds so simple and obvious that you would expect everyone to have in place a comprehensive estate planning program. But in reality, do they? Research shows that only a distressingly few of our producers actually have developed an estate-building plan and are working it.

Why is this? The answer is *default*. The use of the word in this context is intended to suggest an unfortunate condition of human nature. In terms of estate planning, it means failure to take advantage of the opportunities that exist for estate building, failure to meet one's family responsibilities and failure to provide security.

This has something to do with age and experience. When we are earning $800 or $1,000 a month, it is difficult to imagine that the family earning $50,000 or $100,000 has any trouble making ends meet. But the dilemma of the higher-income families is essentially the same if they are not emotionally and psychologically prepared with a functioning estate plan.

Inexperience with handling substantial income is part of the problem. We also mentioned age. Perhaps deep down there is the all-too-human reluctance to accept the inevitability of age and ultimate retirement or, even beyond that, the inevitability of death.

The Romans had an answer to this problem. To remind themselves of their mortality, their heroes retained a "whispering slave," whose function was to follow the hero as he rode in triumph through the street, and to whisper in his ear the truth that all men, even he, must some day get old.

Estate Planning Is Within Your Reach

Perhaps we could all use a whispering slave because the good news is that the means to build and pass on a sound estate are within the reach of every producer in the real estate profession. The main thing is to get started!

Getting started is the difficult part, because of the default factor, high taxation, the high cost of living and the high cost of living high. What should you do to get started? First, consider the following points:

Develop a Plan　In developing your estate-building plan, keep in mind that capital, not income, produces security. Without a plan to produce capital, the $100,000 per year earner is in just as much trouble as the $10,000 per year earner. Income alone doesn't get the job done. That's the disappointing discovery of so many of our high-income producers: They lack a plan to develop capital.

Develop and Retain Capital　Classic estate planning has always started with the following two prime principles:

1. Thrift
2. Sound investment

These still apply, but other elements have been added: tax relief and capital accumulation through fringe benefits. One of the most important features of this program is to free up income for investment, not simply to free up income for a more expensive way of life. This refers to our earlier comment about the high cost of living high.

Establish Estate Planning Objectives　To plan your estate, consider long-term and short-term objectives. In the short term, estate planning provides for the needs of each family member now, while the income earner is active. In the long term, it provides for the same needs of the same people, if and when the planner becomes disabled, retires or dies.

To plan successfully, you must meet present and future goals. This seems simple enough, but from the observations of experts, it sets in motion events that raise deep-seated issues and problems.

Traditionally, establishing a plan to ensure current support and security starts with four elements:

1. Home
2. Income
3. Savings account
4. Life insurance

The manner in which you attack these issues will seriously affect your long-term objectives. Your income and your home, for instance, not only help establish a standard of living, they control the funds available for investment as well. The higher your standard of living, the less you are able to put aside to build an estate. Your standard of living often, in fact, operates to impede or prevent estate building.

Everyone should remember the necessity of maintaining a balance among the four critical short-term objectives: home, income, savings account and life insurance. By determining goals in these areas, you begin your excursion into estate planning, at the same time affecting your performance goals at the office. Your goals form the bedrock needs you must satisfy through your work.

What about future objectives, the long-term goals we referred to earlier? There is no right or wrong set of objectives. They must be personally determined by each individual. One person's set is as good as another's; the point is to have them.

What income do you want your spouse to have available when you die? How much will the rest of the family require? What if you become disabled? Or retire? The answer to these and other questions will determine your objectives. They demand a good deal of thinking through. You must evaluate the needs of each member of the family, remembering any support obligations you may have for relatives outside your immediate family.

You must make lifetime decisions about such things as life-style and standard of living:

- Do you want your children to go to college? To graduate school?
- If so, do you plan to pay the full cost of this education or will you expect your children to help by working or getting scholarship aid?
- Do you want to give them further security by leaving them an inheritance? By transferring part of your estate to them while you're alive? Or do you think it better to send them out in the world to make their own way while you donate to charitable organizations?

Each person's answer to these questions will be different. In addition, they will vary according to age and family custom. Determination of objectives is, as are all parts of estate planning, flexible and continuous. It will change as you change.

Start Now!   The point is to plan now before a large income inflates the standard of living beyond your capability of reversing it.

We suggest you go to any bookstore and buy a book on the subject of estate planning. Some very good ones are available in paperback at a reasonable cost. Any public library should have a section devoted to this subject as well.

What is an estate planning team? Who should be on this team? Again, this is a personal choice, but eventually the service of an attorney, an accountant and a life insurance underwriter will be necessary. As your plan progresses, you may feel the need to include a trust officer and an investment adviser.

In any event, after you have informed yourself to a point, seek advice and help; don't try to do it yourself.

Once your *personal financial plan*, your estate-building program, is underway, you will be in a much better position to set your income targets. It now must be obvious that there will be two levels of goal-setting:

- The income required to take care of your home, your family expenses, your savings program and your life insurance
- The additional income required to establish your plan to produce investment capital

By establishing business development goals to support these personal financial goals, you take full advantage of your sales position. You are truly in business for yourself, and your goals must be perfectly synchronized.

ACTION COMMITMENTS

I have read the previous section and realize I must do the following:

TO DO	TARGET DATE OF COMPLETION	ACTION COMPLETED
1.		
2.		
3.		
4.		
5.		
6. Meet with sales manager.		

2

How To Establish Objectives

Your job and your career as a professional real estate salesperson require that you be goal-oriented. A goal-oriented individual practices a regular discipline—that of setting objectives and then charting the daily activities needed to accomplish those objectives. By following the process set forth in this chapter, you will gain control of your own production and therefore of your own career.

YOUR MISSION, SHOULD YOU CHOOSE TO ACCEPT IT . . .

Achieving the following goals will contribute dramatically to your success as a real estate salesperson:

- Making appointments for planned listing presentations
- Telephone canvassing for listings
- Updating your sphere-of-influence file

- Calling people included in your sphere-of-influence file
- Maintaining a file of FSBOs, and calling them
- Calling MLS expirations
- Recording new births and calling the parents
- Calling transferees and promotions cited in the newspaper
- Calling builders
- Making appointments with "open listings"
- Doing some research for vacant land for development
- Contacting local businesses for possible commercial listings
- Keeping in close touch with former buyers
- Developing contacts with company relocation personnel
- Making weekly contacts with company relocation personnel
- Making weekly contact with your sellers
- Making weekly contact with your current buyers
- Calling other brokers for houses you need
- Sending direct-mail promotional materials to apartment dwellers
- Checking new listings to maintain an updated knowledge of the market
- Canvassing by phone for potential buyers of commercial listings
- Following up your referrals by mail
- Listening to real estate–related or self-improvement audiocassettes
- Reading a book on sales or real estate
- Analyzing your last listing presentation
- Planning tomorrow's activities
- Writing thank-you notes and letters you've been putting off
- Constantly analyzing your work habits

Not only must you achieve the preceding, but you must possess the following qualities.

The ACTION Salesperson

An "action salesperson" exhibits the following traits and qualities:

- The desire, ability, interest, integrity, honesty and tenacity it takes to succeed
- The perception of what is appropriate and pleasing
- A neat appearance
- An even temperament
- Common sense
- An appreciation of a homeowner's emotional needs
- A professional mind
- Interest in people
- Need for a good income
- The ability to influence people
- The will to work long and odd hours
- An eagerness to learn
- Affiliation with social groups, clubs, etc.
- Hobbies and special interests
- Good personal habits (courtesy and punctuality)

ACTION SELF-ANALYSIS

"Honesty is not the first step in greatness; it is greatness in itself."

The first step in establishing objectives is to determine your needs and desires. To do this, complete the following "action self-analysis" as honestly as you can.

1. Why did I decide to become a salesperson? (Answer before reading the next question.)

   _____

   _____

2. What do I like best about my job? _____

   _____

   What do I like least? _____

   _____

3. Which of my friends has a better job? What is that job?_____

   _____

4. Why do I feel that job is better than mine? _____

   _____

5. Would I want my child to be a salesperson? Why or why not?_____

   _____

6. If the world's best salesperson had my job, where I am, what would he or she be able to produce in sales volume? $_____ Personal yearly income? $_____

7. What do I expect to produce next year given my present rate of growth in sales volume and personal yearly income?

   Sales volume: $_____

   Yearly income: $_____

8. How am I different from the "best salesperson" I described earlier? What does he or she do differently? (State at least three things.)

   _____

   _____

   _____

9. Am I guilty of underestimating my potential? Explain.

_____

_____

10. How do I rate myself in these categories, on a scale of one to ten, with one being the lowest?

What is my attitude toward

My job?_____Ambition?_____Goals?_____Enthusiasm?_____

Professionalism?_____Cooperation?_____

Product knowledge?_____Loyalty?_____Self-Image?_____

If you are completely honest in your self-assessment, you can learn about yourself and what you need to do to make yourself better.

The real question is, "Am I humble enough to become great?"

WHAT ARE GOALS?

Goals are objectives or results. A goal is a specific point of completion; it is so specific that upon completion you are aware of its accomplishment, and you can say to yourself, "Yes, I achieved it."

In today's society, most people are not goal-oriented; they are the products of other people's goals. Workers are expected to achieve the goals handed them by their supervisors. These, the company's goals, were handed to the supervisors by management. The consumer is a product of the manufacturer's goals.

Someone else cannot hand you a goal or plan and expect it to work. A goal should and must be identified and developed by the individual who must achieve it.

Today's science of human development has found that most people don't achieve their goals. They blame themselves for not succeeding with such statements as "I set my objectives too high," or "I really didn't want it anyway."

Why did they fail?

- The goal was unrealistic.
- The selected goal was not clearly defined.
- They used an incorrect procedure for establishing the goal.
- They did not include an ACTION plan to achieve the goal.

Why should you set goals?

- You shouldn't and can't unless you want to!
- No plan will have merit unless you are personally committed and want it enough to work for it.
- Your goal has to be something you alone want; no one can establish it for you.

THE ACTION PLAN

Goal-setting is a disciplined skill. It involves a personal commitment and always includes a plan of action.

By setting up an ACTION plan, you determine a goal you want to achieve and lay out a plan to achieve it.

Action Step 1   Analyze your needs. How much do you need to survive financially? Determine how much money you need to meet all normal obligations.

Action Step 2   List your wants. No matter how remote they may seem, list the things you want. They might include a new home, a car, a vacation, a college education and so forth. Perhaps what you want is less tangible: a feeling of self worth, the respect of others, or a sense of freedom, accomplishment or belonging. Try to stretch yourself, while at the same time being honest about what you want. Is it truly attainable? Remember that being attainable does not mean that the goal's attainment must be simple; the goal must, however, be realistic.

Action Step 3   Set your goals. List how much you need. Determine how much is required to attain what you want. Add the two: *Need + Want = Objective.*

Put your objective in writing. This is necessary, because by doing so, you commit yourself to achieving that goal.

Action Step 4   Determine an ACTION plan. What must you do to accomplish your objective? Take your goal (preferably, one established for the upcoming year) and work backwards.

How much money will you have to make each month to accomplish your goal? How many listings each month, at what average price? How many sales each month, at what average price?

How many contacts will you have to make each month, each week, each day, to accomplish your long-term goal? (Contact is defined as communication with prospective or current clients by telephone, through the mail or in person.)

Action Step 5   Convert ACTION plan to daily planning. Once you have determined how many contacts you will need to make, determine how you will make them (through a telephone campaign, by mail, in person). Enter in your daily planning what you want to do each week.

Review your plan every week. What did you do right? What needs to be revised?

Action Step 6   Include checkpoints. Each month, review the previous month's activities and analyze them. Assess your progress and revise your schedule or activities, if necessary.

Write down these review points in your daily planning. Develop a habit of checking your progress regularly. You can determine ahead of time whether you are going to miss your mark and plan what to do to correct it.

MAINTAIN YOUR MOTIVATION

Once you've determined your goal, have a plan of ACTION and have begun a few weeks of activities, how do you maintain that evasive feeling of drive?

Many tasks involved in implementing a plan of ACTION have no immediate reward or payoff. Because of the lack of immediate rewards, many people cannot maintain adequate motivation to complete the steps in their ACTION plan. When this happens, it is often helpful to establish some intermediate rewards as a means of maintaining motivation. In other words, you can develop a self-reward system when "natural" rewards are missing.

The concept of self-reward involves choosing a pleasant experience and using it to reward yourself after you have completed a desired activity. For completing a mail campaign, for example, you might reward yourself by going out to dinner. (Only you can determine what you would consider a reward.) Planning such rewards can help you stay with your plan until it has been completed.

Use the following three general principles for developing a successful reward system:

1. The reward should be consistent. Haphazard rewarding, in which the desired activity is sometimes rewarded and sometimes is not, is less effective than providing a reward each time the activity is performed.

2. The reward should be provided as soon after completing the activity as possible. The point is to associate the reward with completing the desired activity.

3. The reward should be clearly linked to the activity. Being specific about the activity and the reward helps clarify the connection.

SUCCESS BAROMETER

Beginning with yourself and your objectives, make certain you are properly confident about what you need and want to accomplish. Here are some suggestions to use as guides indicating success:

- Confidence—remaining poised in everyday transactions
- Competence—achieving in-depth knowledge of the mechanics of real estate business
- Number of transactions—size is unimportant
- Client loyalty—having made such an impression on at least one customer that he or she has indicated a desire to do repeat business with you
- Smooth and friendly relationships with office and sales staff
- Authority—establishing a reputation for knowledgeability in your chosen area of business
- Integrity—demonstrating that you are reliable
- Superior business service—pride in the service you can offer a client
- Goal orientation—constantly working an ACTION plan, an organized plan with a goal in mind

These must be your distinguishing characteristics if you are to become and remain successful.

Sixty Percent of Your Income Will Come from Listings Sold

The following "ACTION calculator" is based on the premise that, since 60 percent of your income will come from listings, that form of income is all you need to calculate. Once you have derived the number of contacts you must make each day to achieve your goal, the remaining 40 percent from sales will naturally fall into place.

This listing ACTION calculator will enable you to determine the average number of daily contacts you must make to achieve your 12-month goal.

We have worked an example for you below:

1. Your average earnings per listing sold are $1,500.

2. How much money do you want to earn in the next 12 months? For example, let's say you want to earn $50,000. Since listings are 60 percent of your income, we'll calculate this as .6 × $50,000 = $30,000.

3. How many presentations must you make to gain a listing? In this example, the salesperson usually gains a listing after 10 presentations.

4. Divide your earnings per listing sold (line 1) by presentations per listing (line 3). This gives you your earnings per listing presentation: $1,500 ÷ 10 = $150.

5. a. How many contacts must you make to gain a listing? (20) b. Divide your earnings per presentation (line 4, $150) by contacts per presentation (line 5a, 20). This is your earnings per contact. This salesperson must make 20 contacts to gain a listing: $150 ÷ 20 = $7.50.

6. a. Divide your listings earnings goal for the next 12 months (line 2) by 50. This is your listing earnings goal per week: $50,000 ÷ 50 = $1,000. b. Divide the result by 6, depending on the number of working days. This is your listing earnings goal per day: $1,000 ÷ 6 = $166.67.

7. Divide earnings per day, line 6 b, by earnings per contact, line 5 b. This is your required number of contacts per day to

achieve your earnings goal: $167 \div 7.50 = 22$ contacts per day.

▼ ACTION RECALL

How To Establish Objectives

1. Define objectives, goals or end results.
2. You must identify your own goals:
   - Only you can work your goals.
   - You can't work someone else's plan.
3. Four reasons why people may not attain their objectives:
   - Unrealistic goals
   - Weak goal selection
   - Goals not properly established
   - No ACTION plan
4. Six steps in establishing an ACTION plan:
   - Analyze needs
   - List wants
   - Set goals
   - Determine ACTION plan
   - Convert plan to daily planner
   - Include checkpoints
5. Three principles to follow in developing a reward system:
   - Consistent application
   - Prompt reward
   - Reward linked to activity
6. Nine attributes of a successful salesperson:
   - Confidence
   - Competence
   - Knowledge of company history and accomplishments
   - Number of transactions
   - Increased client base
   - Client loyalty
   - Goal orientation
   - Authority
   - Integrity
7. A goal cannot be achieved unless it contains an ACTION plan.

8. Once you have established your ACTION plan, use daily planning to chart and measure your progress.

ACTION COMMITMENTS

I have read the previous section and realize I must do the following:

TO DO	TARGET DATE OF COMPLETION	ACTION COMPLETED
1.		
2.		
3.		
4.		
5.		
6. Meet with sales manager.		

3 The Competitive Market Analysis

One of the most important aspects of getting started is your familiarity with property in your area. Before you can learn all there is to know about the values in your listing bank, you must learn the values of homes in your community to make a comparison.

How many times have people told you what to do without giving you any indication of how to go about it? Here's an example of this type of situation:

A man purchased a very sophisticated computing system. The third day after it was installed, the computer network simply stopped. In his anguish, the man called a systems analyst in to check the system and find exactly what was wrong with it. The systems analyst took a look at the computer, smoked his pipe and walked around the unit a few times, walked in back of it, poked his head over the top of the unit and asked the owner if he had a screwdriver. The owner gave him a screwdriver and the analyst disappeared behind the computer for several minutes.

He then stood up and told the owner to push the start button. The owner did and the computer roared back to life.

The next day the owner received a bill for the systems analyst
. . . $500. The owner shouted "$500! All he did was turn a screw!"
In disgust, he sent the bill back to be itemized.

After a few days, the invoice returned. It now stated,

Repair of computer	$500.00
Turning one screw	.50
Knowing what screw to turn	$499.50

BECOME AN EXPLORER

How many of us miss the boat because we simply don't know
which screw to turn? I would imagine quite a few of us have.

Ways To Improve Your Knowledge of the Marketplace

1. Build into your daily plan tours of all listings held by your
office. Take notes as you tour them; write down amenities
and improvements. Note the price, any faults and how long
each property has been on the market.

    After you have seen a number of listings, you will begin to
see basic similarities that are conducive to value: size, location,
view, pool, any faults in the property and how long it has been
on the market.

2. Start your own in-depth listing bank or farm area for potential business. Here's how:

    • Tour office listings in your listing bank.

    • Tour outside broker listings in your listing bank.

    • Tour any open houses in your listing bank.

    • Research your office transaction files for past sales in your
    listing bank. They are a great source of information for the
    characteristics of a home, amenities, how long it's been on
    the market, original asking price and final sales price.

These sources will help you develop an understanding of
comparable values. By comparing similarities and amenities, you
can usually come up with a basic value. But don't forget to watch
for price and how long a house was on the market; it may have
been overpriced and therefore on the market for a long time.

Compare final selling prices with original asking prices to determine realistic values. For a currently listed house, determine whether you think it could be overpriced compared with other houses with similar characteristics in the immediate area.

It's more difficult to determine similarities in custom one-of-a-kind houses, but do some research from the notes you've taken on these houses. Making lists of the number of bedrooms, extra rooms, any other amenities, custom features, style, price and length of time on the market will help you determine value.

The importance of the comparison method and your familiarity with your listing bank values cannot be overemphasized. You are to become the expert in your listing bank; your clients are going to look to you for guidance when listing their home with you. You must be realistic in placing values. If you overprice their home to appeal to their pride in their home, you run the risk of the home never selling, their eventual mistrust of you and finally losing that client forever. Don't forget: They have neighbors who will hear about their dissatisfaction, and that affects you.

Be sure you keep current with your office inventory. You might not only have a potential client for one of these listings soon, but you must keep current with market trends and values in the entire community because they have a direct impact on your listing bank, too.

As a real estate professional, one of your major functions is that of evaluating property. Salespeople do not give appraisals to clients: We give competitive market analyses.

The primary function of the competitive market analysis (CMA) is to determine a fair price at which to list the property. Through the use of a CMA form, you are able to establish and exhibit your ability as a professional real estate agent.

Earlier in this chapter, we covered the importance of and methods for familiarizing yourself with the current office inventory of listings and your own listing bank.

The primary reason for accomplishing these goals is to build your knowledge of values in your community and in your listing bank. A professional real estate salesperson should strive to be an expert in his or her listing bank for the following reasons:

- Your clients need your expertise because their time is valuable; they are busy pursuing their own careers.
- Your career is real estate; you must therefore attempt to be an authority in your field. Your opinion is your most valuable asset.

- You give a competitive market analysis, or more simply, an opinion . . . but an opinion based on fact.

When prospecting for buyers and sellers, you will sometimes offer to give an evaluation of that person's home. You are offering your services, professionalism, knowledge and expertise, and an evaluation of the home is definitely something the prospective customer is interested in.

Regardless of whether they have considered selling, owners are usually interested in knowing the value of their home; if they express an interest, it's your chance to see the home, as well as talk to the owners to a greater extent to determine whether they are seriously thinking of selling.

The following are the benefits of the CMA:

1. Through the use of the CMA, you are able to establish and exhibit your ability as a professional real estate agent.

2. By using the CMA form, you can provide the owner with a valuable written report concerning the property.

3. The CMA also gives you an opportunity to have direct contact with your client to explain the various selling costs involved in the sale of real estate.

4. The CMA can be used by itself as a means to become better acquainted with owners, or it can be part of the first of two visits:

   - The first, to inspect the property to note its condition and improvements

   - The second—established for later in the day, when both prospects (sellers) are available—to discuss the results of your evaluation

The CMA approach uses five major factors affecting a home's value:

1. Location: the area in which the home is located, the surrounding neighborhood and access to community activities (schools, churches, etc.)

2. Condition: general wear and tear; the better the condition, the higher the value

3. Improvements: what is on the land, improved appearance and amenities

4. Financing trends: whether money is tight or abundant

5. Supply and Demand: overbuilding versus underbuilding

Preparing the CMA Form

The primary function of the CMA is to determine a fair price at which to list the property. The day of consumerism is with us and adequate disclosure early in the listing process is a necessity. The first step in this process is preparation of the CMA.

Action Step 1   Your office probably has a worksheet to use while exploring property to note items of importance. It can be extremely helpful, since few people can remember all items after they've left the home.

- See the property in the daytime, thus seeing the home as the buyers will.
- Inspect the property and use your worksheet to note lights, conditions and improvements.
- Measure rooms, if necessary.
- Once your worksheet is completed, return to your office to prepare your final evaluations.

Action Step 2   Your next step is to gather data on homes comparable to the prospective seller's. This is accomplished through the use of

- Title companies
- Assessor's books
- Your local Board of REALTORS®
- Market data in your own office
- Your own knowledge of the selling price of homes comparable to the prospective seller's.

Action Step 3   Fill in the CMA form. Information on the prospective seller's property is filled in at the top. The comparable properties you have selected are placed in the appropriate "Sold," "For Sale Now" and "Did Not Sell" sections.

The completed CMA form is your statement of facts backing your opinion and recommended selling price. The prospective sellers have the chance to see for themselves their competition and your reasons for your recommendation.

Beware of Possible Conflict

A few words regarding square footage of the home: Most listing forms provide for square footage. It's important to note that, in most areas, the figure you provide must be precise. Therefore, if you do provide this information on a CMA, note in writing that the figures are *approximate*. In this, as in all other areas of real estate agency, it is important to know the requirements in your area. Check with your local Board of REALTORS®.

Also, be sensitive to a prospective seller's emotional feelings toward his or her home. To most people, their home is not only the most expensive, but also the most emotional product they ever purchase. Even if they bought this home to fix up, they've probably put a great deal of time, labor and love and money into it. It is their home.

After your CMA is complete and you are ready to see your clients, remember this: Your clients think their property is worth more than anyone else's. Help them become realistic about the price so it will sell. Don't feed their ego with an unrealistic price just to get the listing.

Do your homework; prove to them the price to sell.

▼ **ACTION RECALL**

Competitive Market Analysis

1. There are four advantages to using the CMA:
   - It demonstrates your credibility.
   - It provides a written report on the property.
   - It provides direct contact with the prospective seller.
   - It is a means of becoming better acquainted with the prospective seller.
2. Location, condition, improvements, financing trends and supply and demand are the major factors affecting home values.
3. In preparing the CMA, your goal is to determine a fair price at which to list the property.
4. By using the CMA, your clients can see for themselves their competition and the reasons for your recommendations.
5. Sources of home market data include the following:

- Your local Board of REALTORS®
- Title companies
- Assessors' books
- Market data in your office
- Your knowledge of comparable homes

6. Do not include the square footage of a home in your CMA.

7. One reason for preparing a CMA is to provide full disclosure for potential buyers as well as sellers.

8. You are not serving your clients well if you agree to list at the price they suggest.

ACTION COMMITMENTS

I have read the previous section and realize I must do the following:

TO DO	TARGET DATE OF COMPLETION	ACTION COMPLETED
1.		
2.		
3.		
4.		
5.		
6. Meet with sales manager.		

4   How To Use the Telephone Powerfully

The telephone is one of the most valuable tools a real estate salesperson has. It's a time-saver and can help you

- develop new prospects.
- obtain new listings.
- obtain referrals.

OVERCOMING FEAR OF THE PHONE

Most people dread using the phone at times, and some actually fear it. To overcome any apprehension you might feel in making or answering a telephone call, ask yourself two questions: First, what are the absolute worst things that could happen to you when talking to a prospective buyer or seller? He or she could

- say no.
- hang up.
- maybe even get angry and hang up.

Result: That's all that will happen . . . nothing worse.

Now take a moment to consider the best things that could happen. The prospective buyer or seller could

- give you an appointment.
- thank you for calling.
- give you a referral.
- be friendly.
- say yes.

Result: Potential income for you.

It's very important to put telephone use in its proper perspective; think of the rewards it can bring you, not the failures.

DEVELOP GOOD TECHNIQUES

Success in real estate sales depends on overcoming the fear of contacting unknown people, understanding the purpose for making the call, and following a plan, keeping in mind what you want to accomplish in each call, and not getting sidetracked.

As long as you have a plan, you have the advantage with each phone call, regardless of whether you are calling or are being called. Remember, the buyer or seller is not prepared with reasons for saying no; he or she may "freeze." But if you are organized, you will be ready and able to overcome it.

When using the telephone as a sales tool, remember the following:

- Install the desire to do it; think of the potential rewards. But remember that a certain percentage of your calls will fail.
- Have a plan. Why are you calling this person? What do you want him or her to do as a result of your call?
- Force yourself to make the first five calls, then build up your momentum.
- Be warm, friendly, natural and polite, and *smile*.

WHO'S THERE?—INCOMING CALLS

Incoming calls are calls made to you from persons responding to advertising in the newspaper, on signs or from mailing campaigns.

This section will cover preparation and techniques for fielding ad calls and sign calls.

Your major concern with an incoming call is to take control of it and get an appointment. In this, organization and preparation are the keys to your success. If you energetically dedicate yourself to learning the following techniques, you will obtain appointments.

Ad Calls: Get Ready, Get Set . . .

Classified ads are designed to make the phone ring: Your goal is to get the caller's name and phone number, and get the appointments.

1. Before the client calls, be prepared: Know what is being advertised, know every property advertised that day and have backup information on each property.

2. Anticipate the caller's questions. Remember, the prospective buyer is usually calling to find out what is wrong with the property, so he or she can eliminate it from consideration. Answer any questions, then ask qualifying questions. Pinpoint what the caller is really seeking; perhaps you have another property that would meet his or her needs better than the one advertised .

3. Use the ACTION recall method presented in this book.

4. Close for an appointment. No amount of organization and preparation will get you an appointment unless you ask for it.

SAMPLE AD CALL

The following is a sample ad call conversation. On the lefthand side are the steps to be aware of to control the call. To the right are sample responses.

STEP 1.   *Identify yourself.*

> *Salesperson:* "This is Bob Salesperson. May I help you?"

STEP 2.   *Listen to request.*

> *Caller:* "I'm calling on your ad, the two-story colonial in today's paper."

STEP 3.   *Acknowledge caller's interest in ad.*

> *Salesperson:* "The ad you have called on is an interesting home."

STEP 4.   *Place on hold.*

> *Salesperson:* "May I place you on hold while I get the advertising file? (Wait for caller's OK.) One moment, please." (Push hold, locate ad file, then . . .)

STEP 5.   *Get name and phone number.*

> (Remove from hold.) *Salesperson:* "Thank you for waiting. My name is Bob Salesperson. May I ask your name, please?" (After obtaining name, immediately ask for phone number.)

Take control (find hot button).

> *Salesperson:* "Ms. Caller, what exactly appealed to you about this home?"

> *Caller:* "I like the style and it sounds interesting; how much is it?"

STEP 6.   *Answer questions and ask a related qualifying question.*

> *Salesperson:* "They are asking $98,000; is that the price range you had in mind?"
>
> *Caller:* "I'm not sure. Tell me, how many bedrooms does this home have?"
>
> *Salesperson:* "There are four bedrooms in this home. May I ask how many there are in your family?"
>
> *Caller:* "We have six. Where is this home located?"

Give general area (major intersection).

> *Salesperson:* "It's in the Willows area, just east of La Salceda; are you familiar with this area?"
>
> *Caller:* "Yes."

STEP 7.   *Trial close*

> *Salesperson:* "I can show it to you now . . . or would 3 P.M. be better for you?" (Wait for an answer!)
>
> *Caller:* "I'm not sure, can you give me the address?"

Trial close

> *Salesperson:* "I would be glad to give you the address, Ms. Caller. However, the owners have requested that we accompany each visitor to their home. Again, I would be most pleased to show it to you now or this afternoon. Which time is more convenient for you?"

Alternate close

> *Caller:* "About 3 P.M."
>
> *Salesperson:* "Fine. To save you time, I will be available to answer any questions you may have about the home. Shall I pick you and Mr. Caller up, or would you prefer coming to our office?" (Wait for an answer.)
>
> *Caller:* "I don't know. I just don't think I have the time. I'll just keep watching your ads and call again."

Final close

Salesperson: "Yes, you can do that. However, during the day I inspect many homes. When I find the right one for you, when can you see it?"

Caller: "I'm not sure. Look Mr. Salesperson, we only want a good buy."

Final close

Salesperson: "As you may know, when a very good home comes on the market, it sells quickly. If an exceptional buy came on the market tomorrow, you would want to see it, wouldn't you?"

Caller: "Yes, but this two-story colonial just doesn't sound like the home for us."

If no appointment has been made, go into the sincerity close.

Salesperson: "Maybe this home is not for you . . . then again, it may be. The only way I can help you is to show you homes and let you tell me your likes and dislikes. After all, it is difficult to determine your true needs over the phone, isn't it?"

Or

Personal service close

Salesperson: "The best way for me to help you select the right home is to stop by with complete information on several homes and discuss your needs with you and Mr. Caller. I can stop by now, or would this evening be better for you?"

Caller: "Well, you've got the appointment. I guess we can see the property at 3 P.M."

STEP 8.   ***Once appointment has been made . . . re-identify yourself, location and time of appointment.***

Salesperson: "Thank you, Ms. Caller, for calling (company name). Again, my name is Bob Salesperson; our address is _____, near _____. I'll be looking forward to seeing you at 3 P.M."

minder: always get the caller's

- Name
- Address
- Telephone number

Ad Calls

Objective:

Get appointment, name, phone and address.

Steps:

- Identify yourself.
- Listen to request.
- Acknowledge caller's interest in ad.
- Put prospect on hold.
- Come back on line. Repeat your name and ask for client's name, then phone number.
- Answer questions—always followed by qualifying questions; close for appointment; reconfirmation of name, phone, time and place; and thank you.

ACTION COMMITMENTS

I have read the previous section and realize I must do the following:

TO DO	TARGET DATE OF COMPLETION	ACTION COMPLETED
1.		
2.		
3.		
4.		
5.		
6. Meet with sales manager.		

Sign Calls: Get Ready, Get Set. . .

When a person calls in response to one of your signs, your objective is to determine the location of the property, get the caller's name and phone number, and get the appointment. As with ad calls, there are four keys to success in fielding sign calls.

1. Prepare ahead of time: Know where signs are located, know every property with signs and have backup information for these properties.

2. Anticipate the caller's questions: Know how to answer them and what qualifying questions you will ask. Pinpoint what the caller is really seeking; perhaps you have another property that would meet his or her needs better than the one he or she is calling about.

3. Use the ACTION recall method presented in this book.

4. Close for an appointment. No amount of organization and preparation will get you an appointment unless you ask for it.

SAMPLE SIGN CALL

The following is a sample sign call conversation. On the lefthand side are the steps to be aware of to gain control of the call. To the right is an example of response.

STEP 1.   *Identify yourself.*

> *Salesperson:* "Bob Salesperson speaking."
>
> *Caller:* "I'm calling about the house with the sign (Gives area or address)."

STEP 2.   *Pinpoint location of sign.*

> *Salesperson:* "We have several signs in this area. Did you notice the address or the nearest cross street?"
>
> *Caller:* "Yes, it's on Willow Street, near Sheila Avenue."

STEP 3.   *Call-back technique to obtain name and phone number.*

> *Salesperson:* "Fine sir. I'll get the information file on this home. My name is Bob Salesperson. At what number can I reach you? . . . Your name please? Are you at home now?" (If not, obtain home number; it helps to identify possible listing call.)
>
> *Caller:* "You can reach me at (xxx)xxx-xxxx."
> *Salesperson:* "I'll be right back with you, Mr. Caller. Thank you for calling."

STEP 4.   *Locate listing information and call back.*

> *Salesperson:* "Mr. Caller?"
>
> *Caller:* "Yes?"
>
> *Salesperson:* "This is Bob Salesperson with the information file on that home, and there is considerable detailed information for you. I can show you the home now or at 4 o'clock. Which would you prefer?

Caller: "Can you give me some information on the phone first?"

STEP 5. *Answer questions.*

Salesperson: "Yes, what information may I help you with?"

Qualifying questions

Caller: "What is the price?"

Salesperson: "They are asking $88,000. Is this the amount you have in mind?"

Caller: "Maybe. Tell me, how large is this home?"

Salesperson: "This home has five bedrooms. May I ask how many there are in your family?"

Caller: "We have seven."

STEP 6. *Trial close*

Alternate choice

Salesperson: "Mr. Caller, in checking my schedule, I have some time to show you this now or at 2:30. Which is better for you?"

Caller: "Well, Mr. Salesperson, this home sounds a little out of our price range, so we'll keep looking for your sign, and if we see something, we'll call."

Final close

Salesperson: "Mr. Caller, when you see this house, you may find it is just what you are looking for. Then again, it may not suit you. The only way I can help you is to show you a home and let you tell me your likes and dislikes. After all, you know it is difficult to determine your true needs over the phone, isn't it?"

Or

Tie down last resort to get name, address and phone number (interim close).

Salesperson: "During the day, I inspect many homes. When I find the right one for you, where can I reach you?"

STEP 7.   *Reconfirm appointment.*

> *Salesperson:* "Thank you, Mr. Caller, for calling. Again, my name is Bob Salesperson; our address is _____. I'll be looking forward to seeing you at 3 o'clock."

Allow Mr. Caller to hang up first.

Reminder: always get the caller's

- Name
- Address
- Telephone number

▼ **ACTION RECALL**   ## Sign Calls

Objective:

To get appointment, name, phone and address.

Steps:

- Identify yourself.
- Pinpoint location of sign and property.
- Call-back technique: Get phone number, locate listing information and call back.
- Answer questions; ask qualifying questions.
- Close for appointment.
- Reconfirm name, phone, time and place.
- Identify yourself again and thank prospect.

ACTION COMMITMENTS

I have read the previous section and realize I must do the following:

TO DO	TARGET DATE OF COMPLETION	ACTION COMPLETED
1.		
2.		
3.		
4.		
5.		
6. Meet with sales manager.		

Ad and Sign Call Objections and Counteractions

It's important to turn the negative into positives; a slightly irrelevant example of this is seen in the story of a little boy and his pet turtle.

The little boy loved this turtle! Every morning before he went to school, he would look in the box where the turtle slept and feed him.

One morning as he started to feed the turtle, he looked into the box and found that the turtle was dead. He began to cry; finally, his father said, "Son, quit crying, go to school, cooperate with the teachers and do your work. Then, at 3:30 when school is over you can invite all your friends in for a real funeral procession.

"Your turtle will be buried in grand style, and as soon as we have the turtle buried, we'll have all your friends in for ice cream and cake. Then, as soon as we finish the cake and ice cream, I'll take all of you to the movies."

The little boy stopped crying and his eyes began to swell to the size of silver dollars. Then, he happened to look down into the box. The turtle he thought was dead was really only sleeping. The little boy looked up at his dad and said, "Let's kill him, Dad."

The true professional can handle situations that arise daily and control them in such a way that we motivate people to do the thing we know should be done.

Reduce to the Ridiculous or Look for the Simplest Solution

Harry Houdini, one of the greatest magicians in the world, thrilled audiences with his miraculous feats of escape from the cells of the strongest jails. The jailer was always bewildered when Houdini would set himself free within a few minutes.

One time, something went wrong. He went to a small town and was directed to the jailer. Houdini challenged the jailer to secure him in a cell. The jailer put him in handcuffs, chained his legs, wrapped his arms in a strait jacket and left him in a cell.

In just a few minutes, Houdini had freed himself of the handcuffs, the chains on his legs and even the strait jacket. Now he was left with the locked door of the cell. He began to work on the cell door. He worked for an hour, two hours and finally with complete exhaustion, leaned against the cell door. It swung open.

The jailer was deeply amused by all these goings on and said, "Harry, I didn't bother to lock the cell door because I knew it wouldn't hold you, anyway."

Houdini forgot to look for the simple solution.

Quite often, we are inclined to look for the difficult solution to solve problems; if we look a little deeper, in most cases we find that the simple solution is really the best. For instance:

- *Where's the property located?*

    "This property is located in the (give general area, followed by. . .) Are you familiar with this area?" *or,* "Is this an area you'd consider?"

- *I'd like the exact address.*

    "I'd be happy to give you the address; however, one of the conditions of our contract with the seller is that we accompany each client to the property. I'm free now, or would 2 P.M. be better?"

- *I'll meet you at the property.*

    If a sign call "Fine, Mr. Buyer, I'll be there in ten minutes. I'll be in a (describe your car). What kind of car are you driving?"

    If an ad call "That would be fine, Mr. Buyer; however, our office isn't far from the property. To avoid the possibility of missing one another, can you come in at 1 P.M. or would 3 P.M. be better?"

- *We would like to just drive by the property.*

    "It's always a good idea to see the exterior of a home as well as the neighborhood. What time do you plan to drive by? Fine, I'll be available at that time to answer any questions you may have about the property. Shall I pick you up, or would you prefer coming to my office?"

    Or

    "Fine, I'll be happy to drive you by the property, Mr. Buyer; however, it would be a shame for you to miss this beautiful backyard (only if it has one). Now, to save you some time, I can show it to you now . . . or would 2 P.M. be better?"

- *How close are the schools?*

    "I'd be happy to show you the exact location of the schools, Mr. Buyer. How old are your children?"

    If the required schools are within walking distance, tell the callers; if they're not, tell them, "We'll measure the distance when we see the home."

    "I can show the home now, or would 2 P.M. be better for you?"

- *How far is the shopping?*

    "I'll be happy to show you the shopping center. Do you drive, or would you have to walk to do your shopping?" If the answer is "I drive," then say, "Well, I'm sure you'll find the shopping center conveniently located. I have some time now, or would 2 P.M. be better for you to see this home?" If the answer is, "I must walk," then say, "Well, I'm sure it's important to you to be within walking distance to shopping. I can show you the home now, or would 4 P.M. be more convenient for you?" If it's not close to shopping, have some alternative properties to show in the shopping area.

- *How much are the taxes?*

    "I think you'll find the taxes are proportionate to the price of the home, Mr. Buyer. What are you paying now?" or "Is this the price range you had in mind?"

Or

"I don't have the exact amount; however, I will obtain it from the assessor before you arrive. Can you come in at 10 A.M., or would after lunch at 1 P.M. be more convenient?"

- *What is the loan on this property?*

"Are you planning to assume a low interest loan, Mr. Buyer? What did you have in mind for your initial investment?"

Or

"This loan on this property is quite low, Mr. Buyer. What did you have in mind for your initial investment?"

- *What is the down payment?*

"They're asking $_____. What did you have in mind for your initial investment?"

Or

"On this home, the down payment would be $_____. Is that about what you had planned on? Mr. Buyer, may I ask if we found a home that was exactly what you were looking for, or even better, how large an initial investment would you make in order to become the owner of such a home?"

- *Are there any children in the area?*

"I think it would be difficult to find an area that didn't have any children. How many children are there in your family, Mr. Buyer?"

- *Why are they selling?*

"I don't have the personal file on my desk, Mr. Buyer. Another salesperson is using it. I'll be happy to obtain that information and call you back. At what number can I reach you?" Never say the home is too large or too small.

- *What is the price of the home?*

"They are asking $_____. Is this about the price range you had in mind?"

- *Will the owners take less?*

"I've learned never to make a decision for a client, Mr. Buyer. However, would you be interested in buying it if they will?"

Or

"I'm not sure, Mr. Buyer. Have you seen the home? We have shown this property to many people since the ad appeared. The consensus seems to be in favor of the price, and we expect a sale soon. However, the first offer may buy it. Can you see it now, or will 4 P.M. be better?"

Or

"Would you like to purchase the home if they would take less?"

- *My (wife/husband) will take a look and screen the home.*

    "This is one method of looking at homes, Mr./Ms. Buyer. However, I think you'll agree that the purchase of a home is one of the largest investments most people will make. I know I would never want to place a responsibility such as this on my spouse. I'd be happy to show both of you this home after you get off work, or would Saturday be more convenient?"

    Or

    "I can appreciate how you feel, Mr./Ms. Buyer. I'm sure you're attempting to save time. However, with a home that is getting as much activity as this one, would your spouse be able to purchase it, should it be the home for you, before someone else does?" (Close for appointment.)

- *I don't have time to look with you.*

    "I understand your time is important, Mr. Buyer, as is my own. And, I'm sure you'll agree that it's impossible to purchase a home over the phone. So, to save us both time, I'll set up a showing of the property that will take but a few minutes of your time, at your convenience. Would this afternoon be all right, or would this evening, say 8 P.M., be better for you?"

    Or

    "Buying a home is probably the most important purchase you'll make. I'm sure you're aware that proper guidance could save you both time and money. I'll be happy to meet with you now, or would 2 P.M. be better?"

    Or

    "I understand your frustration. Buying a home is an important decision, one that requires much time. When you are busy, time is hard to find. Printed information on several homes, as well as professional guidance, can save you time and money. I'll be happy to drop this information to you, Mr. Buyer. What is your address? (Wait for response.) Your phone number?"

- *How long has it been for sale?*

    "I couldn't say for sure, Mr. Buyer. However, I'll be glad to obtain that information for you. How long have you been looking for a home? (Wait for response.) I see. Well, if this just happened to be the right home for you, I'm sure you wouldn't want to miss seeing it, would you? (Wait for response.) Well, then, I can show it to you now, or would 4 P.M. be better for you?"

- *I want a modern home. Is this modern?*

    "Mr. Buyer, I've found that different people describe homes in different ways. Probably the best way for me to help you would be to show it to you and have you tell me just what it is you're looking for in a home. I'm free now, or would 2 P.M. be more convenient?"

    Of course, if it is the style they've said they want, tell them so, then close for the appointment.

- *How far is it from a freeway?*

    "This home is quite convenient to the freeway, Mr. Buyer. Where do you work?"

- *I can't come in today.*

    "Fine, Mr. Buyer. Tomorrow would be more convenient for me, as well. Would tomorrow morning fit into your schedule or would the afternoon be better?"

    Close, using alternate choice of time.

    ### Or

    "Are you off on Saturday or Sunday? Fine. I can show you the property at 1 P.M. or 4 P.M. on Sunday. Which do you prefer?"

- *I'll call you back rather than give my name and telephone.*

    "That's fine. However, I spend a large portion of my time out of the office showing and inspecting homes. Should we be unable to make contact again, and providing this is the home for you, you would want to know more about it, wouldn't you?"

ACTION COMMITMENTS

I have read the previous section and realize I must do the following:

TO DO	TARGET DATE OF COMPLETION	ACTION COMPLETED
1.		
2.		
3.		
4.		
5.		
6. Meet with sales manager.		

HONEST . . . IT'S NOT AN OBSCENE CALL!—OUTGOING CALLS

Telephone prospecting generates business in a different way. Consider the story of the sultan who was 100 years of age.

The sultan had 30 wives. Each morning he would awaken and decide which wife he wanted to live with that day, and then he would send for his runner, a ten-year-old boy, to pick up the wife and bring her back to the old sultan.

When evening came, the young runner would return the wife to where she resided. This continued every day for the next 30 years, at the end of which the old sultan was 130 years old, and the runner 40. The runner dropped over dead from cardiac arrest!

It all goes to show that business is good for all of us, but it's the running after it that really kills us!

Telephone prospecting will not kill us. It assists us in closing a higher percentage of the daily contacts we make. Telephone prospecting can be a definite advantage to you because it doesn't cost you anything. It saves time, and you can work the percentages.

If you energetically apply yourself to learning and using the techniques set forth in this chapter, you will obtain more appointments and thereby obtain more listings. If you organize yourself and follow a written plan, your success will definitely increase.

After you have completed this section, you should be able to

- Describe the objective for making prospecting calls.
- List the six steps to take to organize your skills.
- Describe why most clients want to say no.
- List two examples of a thinking question.
- List at least three approaches you can use with new prospects.

Outgoing calls are those you make to prospects, either while prospecting in your listing bank or when following up on mailing campaigns to potential clients. Your objective is to find the client who is interested in selling or buying; to obtain information about neighbors possibly selling their homes; to establish rapport with this person for future business; and to close for an appointment.

Organize

As in every aspect of real estate sales, you have a major need to be organized when telephone prospecting.

Action Step 1   Have the cards of people you plan to call in front of you.

Action Step 2   Have a specific reason for calling.

Action Step 3   Anticipate objections the prospective buyer or seller might have.

Action Step 4   Know how to answer these objections and ask qualifying questions about his or her real needs.

Action Step 5   Close for an appointment. You'll never get an appointment unless you ask for it.

Action Step 6   Build a file for each home. Record any pertinent data received over the phone on cards for future reference.

The Psychology of the Call

Your objective is to understand that people instinctively want to say no; to distract them by asking a thinking question; and to determine the person's future needs.

Most people you contact already receive many unsolicited phone calls and have built in an almost automatic reflex to say no. You can be certain that you're not the first real estate agent to call them.

In addition, the public is further numbed by exposure to a tremendous amount of selling over the radio and television, stores, on signs and many other forms of media.

To overcome this, distract them by asking a thinking question, such as, "How long have you lived in the area?" "Are any of your neighbors thinking of selling?" "Do you like the area?" "Do you have any friends or relatives who might consider a move into your area?"

Then, determine the owner's future needs. Don't hang up until you explore the possibility of his or her needing your services in the future. The owners may not be thinking of selling right now, but maybe they'll move next year. Offer your help in any of their real estate needs, now or in the future.

Techniques and Suggested Language

Volume Calling

"Mrs. Owner this is Bob Salesperson of Sunny Real Estate. I'm calling this evening to see if you and Mr. Owner are considering selling your home."

"Do you know of any of your neighbors who are thinking of selling?"

"By the way, when will you be selling?"

"Ms. Owner, this is Bob Salesperson of Sunny Real Estate. Our firm represents several people interested in buying property in the neighborhood, and we're checking to see what might be available. Do you know of anyone who may be considering selling?"

Direct Mail Follow-up

"I recently sent some information to you and wanted to answer any questions you might have regarding your real estate needs." (Lead into asking if they want to sell.)

Specific Situation

"Ms. Owner, this is Bob Salesperson of Sunny Real Estate. I have a fine client, a doctor and an attorney with an eight-year-old daughter, who hope to settle in your neighborhood. We would like to help them find a home in your area, since they like it so well. Can you tell me if any of your neighbors have been considering selling?" (Use only if situation is real.)

Sold Cards Follow-Up

"Ms. Owner, this is Bob Salesperson of Sunny Real Estate. I thought you'd be interested to know the home down the street at 12 Michelle has been purchased by Mr. and Mrs. Buyer. They'll be moving in August 15th with their eight-year-old daughter. In the process of selling this home, Mrs. Owner, we were fortunate enough to have come in contact with another nice couple who would like to settle in your neighborhood. Would you tell me if any of your neighbors have been considering selling?"

Just Listed Follow-Up

"Ms. Owner, this is Bob Salesperson of Sunny Real Estate. We just listed a home in your neighborhood, and I thought you might like to have the opportunity to select your new neighbor. Do you have any friends or relatives that might like to move into your neighborhood?"

Calling For Sale By Owner Ads

(See Chapter 3.)

▼ **ACTION RECALL**

Prospecting Calls

Objective:

To find the customer who is interested in selling or buying, and to get an appointment.

Steps:

- Organize; have a plan.
- Have a reason for calling.

- Anticipate objections.
- Know how to answer objections.
- Ask qualifying questions.
- Close for appointment.

Suggested Language:

> "I'm calling this evening to see if you and Ms. Owner are interested in selling your home."
> "Do you know of any neighbors who are thinking of selling?"
> "I recently mailed some information to you and would be happy to answer any questions you may have regarding your real estate needs."

> *Close:* "The best way for me to help you is to drop by to discuss your real estate needs and to prepare a competitive market analysis for your home. I have some free time at 3 P.M., or would 8 P.M. be better?"

ACTION COMMITMENTS

I have read the previous section and realize I must do the following:

TO DO	TARGET DATE OF COMPLETION	ACTION COMPLETED
1.		
2.		
3.		
4.		
5.		
6. Meet with sales manager.		

PROSPECTING CALL OBJECTIONS AND COUNTERACTIONS

The following are some objections you might hear from a client and suggested phrases to help you overcome them:

- *We just bought.*

    "I see. How long ago did you move into the neighborhood?"

    Or

    "Well, now that you're settled (or getting settled), have you any friends or relatives who might be considering a move into the area?"

    Or

"Thank you very much, Ms. Owner. Should you have any questions about this area, please feel free to call me. I'll be happy to be of service in any way I can. My name again is Bob Salesperson, with Sunny Real Estate, and our office is just a phone call away at 555-4567."

- *No, not at present.*

    "Very good, Ms. Owner. I'd like to thank you for your time. By the way, since you've been nice enough to talk to me, we have a number of good buys in homes in the area. Do you have any friends or relatives who have been thinking of buying?"

    If the answer is yes, of course follow through for name and phone number. If no,

    "Thank you, again, Ms. Owner. This is the area I have chosen to be my specialty, so I'll be checking with you from time to time. If ever you have a question concerning real estate, please feel free to call me. I would like to be of service to you."

- *We're renting.*

    "I see. How long have you been renting? Have you considered buying a home?"

    Obtain an answer; if yes, close for appointment to discuss needs.

- *We're planning to buy next year.*

    "Well, then, you've got the right idea, Ms. Buyer. But, do you realize that the home you buy today at today's price and interest rates most likely will cost you two or three thousand dollars more next year, and you'll probably pay a much higher rate of interest for any loan you may require in the purchase of that home? We have a consultation service that we offer at no cost to you, Ms. Prospect. If I can show you how you can actually save money through the purchase of a home now over the prospect of waiting until next year, I'm sure that would be of interest to you, wouldn't it?"

    "Fine, Ms. Buyer. I'll be more than happy to drop over in the evening when Mr. Buyer is home. Would this evening around 7 P.M. be all right, or would tomorrow evening fit better into your schedule?"

- *Taxes are too high.*

    For renters: "I'll have to agree that we pay plenty of taxes, Ms. Buyer. However, in your present status, do you realize that you're paying the taxes for someone else—your landlord?"

"If I can show you the tremendous tax savings you'll gain just from home ownership, Ms. Buyer, I'm sure this would be of interest to you. Wouldn't it?"

"Fine, Ms. Buyer. I'll be more than happy to drop over in the evening when Mr. Buyer is home. Would this evening about 7 P.M. be all right, or would tomorrow evening fit better into your schedule?"

PERSONAL TELEPHONE USE CHECKLIST

Check "yes" or "no" for each answer.

Considerations:

Yes   No

❏   ❏   1. Do I know exactly and specifically the purpose of calls?

❏   ❏   2. Do I have a set plan for making the call?

❏   ❏   3. Am I prepared? Am I organized?

❏   ❏   4. Do I use ACTION recalls?

❏   ❏   5. Do I keep my objective in mind, or do I get sidetracked?

❏   ❏   6. Do I gain control by asking qualifying questions?

❏   ❏   7. Do I answer questions with qualifying questions?

❏   ❏   8. Do I close for the appointment?

❏   ❏   9. Is my voice warm, friendly and relaxed?

❏   ❏   10. Do I communicate to the prospective buyer or seller the advantage of making an appointment with me?

❏   ❏   11. Do I smile when talking?

❏   ❏   12. Do I talk too fast?

Yes **No**

❑ ❑ 13. Do I pace myself and enunciate clearly?

❑ ❑ 14. Am I too brief and curt?

❑ ❑ 15. Do I really listen to what the client is saying?

❑ ❑ 16. Do I interrupt?

❑ ❑ 17. If I receive a call when I'm involved in something, do I convey annoyance?

❑ ❑ 18. Am I too talkative and take too much time?

❑ ❑ 19. Do I sound "canned" or do I sound original?

❑ ❑ 20. Have I tried recording my voice during calls so I can hear how I sound?

❑ ❑ 21. Do I maintain control and interview the client, or does the client interview me?

❑ ❑ 22. When answering my phone, do I say, "(your name) speaking? May I help you?"

❑ ❑ 23. Do I sound warm, natural and friendly?

❑ ❑ 24. Do I say, "thank you"?

ACTION COMMITMENTS

I have read the previous section and realize I must do the following:

TO DO	TARGET DATE OF COMPLETION	ACTION COMPLETED
1.		
2.		
3.		
4.		
5.		
6. Meet with sales manager.		

5 How To Direct Your Time

"No man need live a minute longer as he is because the creator endowed him with the ability to change himself."
—James Cash Penney

The essence of time management is knowing what you need and want to accomplish (goal-setting), and disciplining yourself to accomplish it.

By disciplining yourself, you will recognize what "ready time" and "money time" are, and organize your activities around them. Successful and profitable use of your time requires you to identify different types of time, set priorities, use a daily planner and follow it.

TIME MANAGEMENT

Time management means nothing until you know what you need and want to accomplish. We covered goal-setting in Chapter 2.

Turn to it now if you haven't already set your goals. You can plan your daily activities down to the finest detail, but it will mean nothing unless you know why you're planning and what you want to accomplish.

Two Kinds of Time

Most authorities on time usage in real estate will tell you there are two kinds of time: ready time and money time.

Ready time is the time you spend analyzing your listing bank, making phone calls for appointments, preparing presentations, training and the other tasks that lead to effective use of money time. Ready time is the time you spend preparing and organizing yourself.

Money time is the time you spend with someone who can make a decision. This is the time you spend face-to-face with an actual buyer or seller.

Keep in mind that each type of time is dependent on the other:

- The time you spend preparing your listing bank, making effective use of the telephone, building knowledge of the current market is wasted unless you have a client.
- The time you spend with a client is wasted unless you have the knowledge and skills to meet the client's needs.

Each is vital, but overemphasis on one will eliminate your effectiveness in the other.

Planning

Your objective is to translate your goals into the daily activities you need to accomplish to reach your goals; to set priorities; to build an inflexibility.

Action Step 1   Set your annual goals.

Action Step 2   Discuss them with your sales manager and set short-term objectives.

Action Step 3   Convert these objectives into weekly activity. Use a daily planner.

Action Step 4   Plan each week on the preceding Saturday afternoon or Sunday morning and review the previous week. Look back and evaluate your week; what did you do right?

Action Step 5   Plan daily work the night before.

- Assign priorities every day.
- Most of us have more energy in the morning, so do things you like least in the morning and assign the tasks you like best for afternoon.
- Ask yourself what time(s) of the day you're going to make telephone calls. How many calls are you going to make?
- How much time and what time of the day are you going to devote to your supportive tasks? Supportive tasks include building listing bank files, mailings, updating mailing lists and preparing for listing presentations, competitive market analyses and so on.
- When are you going to tour properties?
- Provide for flexibility. What if something comes up? What would you change or move around?

As you make out your schedule, think of time as opportunity and money. Keep in mind the following:

Major goal: Face-to-face time with prospects and clients.

Assumptions: Out of 52 weeks in the year, six will be involved in vacations, illness, holidays, emergencies and so on, leaving 46 weeks.

46 weeks × 6-day week = 276 days

Out of a nine-hour day, three hours will be spent in travel, administrative detail and meals, leaving six hours of effective work time each day.

Goals versus Hours: If one's goal is a $60,000 annual income, then each effective hour is worth more than $36.

Four Time-Wasting Foes

1. *Busy Work.* Doing trivial, minor or unnecessary jobs. Is what you're doing going to pay off?
2. *Procrastination.*
   Reasons:

- Insufficient interest in the task
- Fear of failure
- Dislike of the task

Solutions:
- Decide what is actually involved.
- Decide who will do the task—you or someone else.
- Set a definite completion date *and stick to it*.

3. *Excuses*.

   Solution: Do it, or forget it!

4. *Regrets*.

   Solutions:
   - Concentrate on today's tasks.
   - "Finish each day and be done with it."—Emerson

Real estate is the highest paid hard work or the lowest paid *easy work*.

Plan your Work and Work Your Plan. The following pages are examples of tasks set forth by a new salesperson during the first month. It could help you set up your own calendar.

ACTION TASK SCHEDULE

A Suggested Schedule for the First Month
Objectives for Week
- Begin to set up listing bank.
- Learn office inventory.
- Pick one FSBO, preferably in your area, on whose home you will make a planned campaign of follow-up visits and calls to obtain the listing.

Daily Tasks
- Drive area of responsibility to check marketing activity.
- Be prepared to critique your impressions of other salespersons at the open houses. What did they do that you liked? Disliked?
- Visit open houses in your own or other areas. List addresses.
- Visit open houses every day.
- Tour office to learn where supplies, files, signs and so on, are kept. Learn other office procedures.

- Review National Association of REALTORS® Salesman's Handbook.
- Lunch: Drop by a friend's home and tell him or her about your entering real estate.
- Make appointments to preview two homes now on the market in your area. Arrange to preview three more office listings you have not seen (or other broker's listings).
- Visit local Board of REALTORS®. Join Board and take orientation and ethics exam. Pick up lockbox key and sign application, where applicable.
- Drop by and call one FSBO in the area to introduce yourself. Try to see that home or set up an appointment to come back.
- Design a schedule of callbacks on this FSBO.
- Plan next day's activities.
- At home, begin to prepare a mailing list of friends, relatives and other associates to whom you wish to mail announcement cards.
- Prepare a listing on your home including advertising directive listing folder. Prepare a seller's net sheet on the listed price.
- Attend office meeting and preview of homes.
- Caravan new office listings.
- Have lunch with a friend and ask for a referral lead.
- Organize your listing bank.
- Work on announcement cards.
- Call FSBO you contacted yesterday; thank him or her for the opportunity of meeting and/or seeing the home (if you did). Make an appointment to see the home if you did not, or to come in the evening with information.
- Work on a competitive market analysis (CMA) for your FSBO or for your area.
- Make list or "hot sheet" of best buys in several price ranges.
- See FSBO.
- Write up a possible contract on one of the listings you have seen; prepare a buyer's cost sheet.
- Check newspapers for possible clients—FSBO work.
- TAKE A DAY OFF!! YOU DESERVE IT!
- Follow up and complete assignments from other days.

At this point, you should have accomplished the following:

- Developed a sample listing of your own home
- Completed area lists
- Developed sample contracts on two homes

- Have a "best buy list" of homes in several price ranges
- Prepared a CMA
- Made 80 contacts in your area
- Called on at least three FSBOs
- Talked to several friends and asked for referrals
- Followed up on clients in newspapers
- Set up your supplies
- Joined local Board and Multiple Listing Service
- Mailed announcement cards to friends, relatives and associates. Try repeating again in the second week.

Third Week Objectives

- Two listing presentations, three showings, listing bank follow-up.
- Mail thank-you notes to persons attending your open house.
- Call any who were possible buyers for the open house or another home. Set up appointments.
- Get FSBOs from the Sunday paper; get appointments.
- Do mail-outs to your listing bank; record them.
- Make 20 follow-up calls to area homes that have received mailers or that you have visited; record them.
- Work on CMA and area file information.
- Call any who were possible buyers for the open house or another home. Set up appointment.
- Make 20 door-to-door contacts in your listing bank.
- TAKE A DAY OFF! Wow, do you ever need it . . .
- Do mail-outs.
- Make follow-ups.
- Make phone calls.
- Knock on doors in your listing bank.
- Close for the appointment.
- Make listing presentations.
- Show property.
- Talk to people for referrals.
- Give out your business cards to everyone.
- Hold an open house.

REPEAT!! REPEAT!!

Don't Quit

When things go wrong, as they sometimes will,
When the road you're trudging seems all uphill,
When the funds are low and the debts are high,
And you want to smile, but you have to sigh,
When care is pressing you down a bit—
Rest if you must, but don't you quit.

Life is queer with its twists and turns,
As every one of us sometimes learns,
And many a person turns about
When they might have won had they stuck it out.
Don't give up, though the pace seems slow—
You may succeed with another blow.

Often the struggler has given up when he might
Have captured the victor's cup;
And he learned too late when the night came down,
How close he was to the golden crown.
Success is failure turned inside out—
So stick to the fight when you're hardest hit—
It's when things seem worst that you *must not quit*.
—Author Unknown

CREATIVE FLOOR TIME HABITS

Time, obviously, is relative. Two weeks on a vacation is not the same as two weeks on a diet.

Floor time is the chance to utilize this opportunity and to be well organized and prepared for

- new prospects calling in on ads.
- new prospects calling in on signs.
- new prospects walking in.
- best utilization of spare time while occupying floor time.

Being prepared and organized is just as important while filling floor time as it is in all areas of your profession.

It is important to be prepared to answer ad and sign calls before you fill your floor time rather than frantically organizing during floor time. Do your research and plan ahead—use your daily planner to build in your preparation time before your floor time.

Since we have covered the techniques of ad and sign calls in Chapter 4, this chapter will focus on walk-ins and creative use of spare time.

Walk-ins

Your objective is to greet the customer courteously; to begin qualifying and determining his or her needs; and to show property.

1. *Greet the customer.* When a customer walks into your office, he or she is usually ready to see property; greet the customer immediately and graciously. Introduce yourself, offer your business card to both husband and wife, if both are present.

2. *Arrange for a backup salesperson to take floor time and go to a conference room.* Be hospitable to your guests; offer them coffee, etc. Don't rush them . . . your time is their time.

3. *Begin qualifying and determining needs.* Integrate questions with normal conversation so as not to sound like an interrogation. Determine what the buyers need, want and are financially capable of affording. If the buyers are new to the area, begin an education of what areas there are. See ACTION recall, later in this chapter.

4. *Show property.* Arrange appointments to show about three homes. Begin gradually to determine further the customers' needs and to assess their reactions when they see these homes. Keep in mind what they say they want may be quite different from what they *really* want. Further qualify them in the car and while showing the homes. See Chapter 10 for more specific techniques.

▼ **ACTION RECALL**   ## Walk-in Sequence

Objective:

Greet customer, qualify and show property.

Steps:

- Greet customer; introduce yourself, give business card(s).
- Arrange for backup salesperson and go to conference room; offer customer coffee, etc.
- Begin qualifying.
- Arrange appointments to show homes.

- Further qualify in car.
- Show homes.

Spare Time

Your objective is to identify possible spare time and make it work for you. Take this opportunity to accomplish tasks that could take time later when you don't have it to spare.

There are periods during your floor time when the phone is quiet and you have the perfect opportunity to use this spare time.

Let's face it. There'll be "one of those days" when nothing happens; the phone won't ring and no one will come into the office. What is there to do? Let's hope that, while preparing for ad calls, sign calls and walk-ins, you also prepared some ideas for making the most of your spare time. Here are a few suggestions:

- Update mailing lists.
- Update and plan mailing program.
- Prepare and address mailing pieces.
- Plan telephone follow-up to mailing pieces.
- Update your listings.
- Work on your daily planner.
- Reread chapters in this book you feel you need to review.
- Review your activities over the past few weeks. What did you do right? What do you need to correct?
- Do any preparation needed for a CMA or offer.
- Scan the newspaper for FSBO ads. Plan how to contact the owners.

Plan your work and work your plan. How you use your time and how well you plan it will determine the quality of the results.

Success is not a destination; it's a continuous journey fulfilling one achievement after another.

ACTION COMMITMENTS

I have read the previous section and realize I must do the following:

TO DO	TARGET DATE OF COMPLETION	ACTION COMPLETED
1.		
2.		
3.		
4.		
5.		
6. Meet with sales manager.		

6 Prospecting— Expanding Your Sphere of Influence

The successful salesperson doesn't pick the skills to pursue based on personal preference; this salesperson balances activity, and manages his or her territory and listing bank.

Knowing what you should be doing and how to do it will help you achieve success. Consider the example of the two shoe salesmen.

Both went to Africa to open up new territories. Three days after their arrival, the first salesman sent a cable to his office: "Returning next plane; can't sell shoes here . . . everybody goes barefoot."

Nothing was heard from the other salesman for about three weeks. Then a thick letter was received by his home office. It said: "Sixty-five orders enclosed, the prospects here are unlimited . . . Nobody here has shoes!"

HOW TO GENERATE FUTURE BUSINESS

In the next few chapters, specific listing and selling skills will be described with pointers on techniques. Listing bank management involves performing all these skills in an organized and intentional fashion. The balance of this book will discuss even more skills; these, too, have to be used in order to manage your listing bank properly.

Listing bank management should be defined as

- Assessing your skills and applying them when you should
- Being responsible for all activities in your listing bank—keeping track
- Taking control of your job: controlling your time, energy and activities
- Planning and anticipating rather than waiting until the crisis occurs.

Planning Activities

- Determine what you need and want.
- Determine what you have to do to achieve what you want.
- Organize your time carefully.
- Follow your plan.
- Tour properties.
- Develop a mail program.
- Use the telephone as a constructive tool.
- Keep a current record of properties in your area.
- Be constantly familiar with the homes and their values in your listing bank.
- Use your floor time constructively.
- Get to know personally as many owners in your listing bank as possible.
- Always be conscious of how you can fill a customer's needs.
- Balance your activities; always be aware of what you are doing and why.
- Balance your production; don't concentrate just on sales and run out of listings, or the opposite.

THE ACTION NEIGHBORHOOD DIRECTORY

Wisdom is knowing what to do next; *skill* is knowing how to do it; *virtue* is doing it.

By creating an ACTION neighborhood directory you can reap countless benefits. First, it's an excellent ice breaker when door-knocking. Second, it's an A-1 way to get acquainted with everyone in your listing bank. Performing a service for them will help them remember you and your company.

An ACTION neighborhood directory also provides benefits for the residents of your listing bank. For instance, it assists residents in finding part-time or temporary help not ordinarily advertised. It also provides help to the teenagers, senior-citizens and others to secure part-time employment.

The cover of your ACTION neighborhood directory should read as follows:

- Heading: "ACTION Neighborhood Directory of Services"
- Your name
- Your company name and phone number
- Your home phone number

The contents of your ACTION neighborhood directory should be as follows:

1. Page 1, "Introductory Letter" (See Sample A)
2. Part-time occupational listings:
   - Services (baby-sitter, yard care, pet care, etc.)
   - Products (Avon, Amway, etc.)
   - Professionals (tutors, accountants, teachers, etc.)
3. Lined page for recipient's personal phone numbers
4. Ages of children and teenagers
5. "Protect your home" (information to help prevent burglaries)

SAMPLE A: INTRODUCTORY LETTER

Dear Friends:

This handy ACTION Directory of Neighborhood Services has been distributed to each home in this area to provide information of temporary or part-time services offered. All individuals listed live in your immediate area.

Many area teenagers and adults offer special home-oriented talents and services for your convenience. Please call on them when you need help!

In preparing this directory, I attempted to contact each homeowner in this area. If you were not home when I called on you, and you or a member of your family has a service to offer, please call me so you will be included in our next edition. I may be reached at the Sunny Realty office or at my residence. Please see covers for my numbers.

Cordially,

_____
(signature)

6. If emergency phone numbers are used, double-check to *make certain they are correct for your entire listing bank.* If your area crosses jurisdictional boundaries, be *very sure* you are using applicable numbers.

7. Information not to be included:
   - Historical or statistical data
   - Listings of government and civic agencies, special groups, churches and schools, etc.
   - Maps
   - "Want Ads," i.e., pets or merchandise for sale. Also "Help Wanted," since it will soon be outdated.
   - Recipes
   - Hobbyists, unless they relate to occupations. (If you include hobbyists, make sure this section is smaller than that for part-time help.)

SAMPLE B: LEGAL DISCLAIMER

The foregoing persons have volunteered the information for their listing in this directory, and no investigation has been made of the person by myself or my company, Sunny Realty. None of the listed persons is an employee of Sunny Realty, with the exception of the party providing this directory. Services rendered by any of the persons listed in the directory are a private matter between the listing agent and the person using the service.

SAMPLE C: LEGAL RELEASE

I/We, the undersigned, do hereby consent to the use of the following information in a neighborhood service directory to be published periodically by Sunny Realty. I/We understand that said directory will be circulated to local residents and businesses and that I will not be compensated for such use. All persons listed under the age of 18 years shall require the signature of a parent or guardian.

Specialty	Name	Address
Phone	Age (if under 18)	Signature
Specialty	Name	Address
Phone	Age (if under 18)	Signature

Note: Since laws vary from state to state, make sure to consult your legal adviser before using this form.

Reminder: The purpose of your ACTION neighborhood directory of services is to assist residents in securing part-time or temporary help.

Legal Protection

Make sure to include a disclaimer: The last item in your directory should be worded as shown in Sample B.

Make sure each person included in your directory signs a legal release. The form you use for soliciting service listings (Sample C) is to be signed in your presence by each person listed in your directory. For persons under the age of 18 years, make sure to obtain the signature of a parent or guardian. Do not ask signee to mail the form to you nor include the form in your directory.

Preparation for Printing

1. It is best to use a computer and high-quality printer for preparing the directory. If you use a typewriter, your directory must be typed letter-perfect with fresh, black ribbon and clean type. Faint typing will not reproduce properly. Erasures must be made expertly. Otherwise, the smudge will be more obvious on the printed page.

2. Assemble your occupations listings in alphabetical order.

3. Number pages at the bottom, on the center of each page.

4. On the rear cover, within boxed border, include the words, *Compliments of:*

   - Your name

   - Your company name

   - Your office phone number

   - Your home phone number

5. Inside the rear cover, include the heading, "Frequently called numbers," followed by several lines for writing by residents.

LISTING BANK MANAGEMENT CHECKLIST

Check "yes" or "no" for each answer.

Yes   **No**

☐   ☐   1. Do I set goals for myself?

☐   ☐   2. Do I know how many contacts I need to make on a daily or weekly basis to achieve my goal?

☐   ☐   3. Do I have a plan to use?

☐   ☐   4. Do I have my plan converted to my daily planner?

☐   ☐   5. Do I follow my plan?

☐   ☐   6. Do I tour properties every week?

☐   ☐   7. Do I frequently drive my listing bank to look for new For Sale signs?

☐   ☐   8. Am I always current with the values of homes in my listing bank?

☐   ☐   9. Do I have a mail campaign?

☐   ☐   10. Do I keep my mailing lists current?

☐   ☐   11. Do I follow up my mailings with phone calls?

☐   ☐   12. Do I see to it that I mail a variety of items to my listing bank and not always the same thing?

☐   ☐   13. Do I have a door-to-door calling plan for my listing bank?

☐   ☐   14. Do I make notes on my listing bank file cards whenever I have made contact with owners, either by mail, phone or in person?

☐   ☐   15. Do I use ACTION recalls when using the telephone?

☐   ☐   16. Do I close for an appointment when on the telephone?

☐   ☐   17. Do I use the personal telephone checklist periodically? (See Chapter 4.)

Yes	No		
❑	❑	18.	Do I offer to make competitive market analyses on owners' homes?
❑	❑	19.	Do I keep a record of mailings to my listing bank and what was sent?
❑	❑	20.	Am I always prepared for my floor time?
❑	❑	21.	Am I prepared for a walk-in client?
❑	❑	22.	Do I know how to qualify a buyer?
❑	❑	23.	Do I know how to counter objections?

What is your plan of action if you have any nos?

ACTION COMMITMENTS

I have read the previous section and realize I must do the following:

TO DO	TARGET DATE OF COMPLETION	ACTION COMPLETED
1.		
2.		
3.		
4.		
5.		
6. Meet with sales manager.		

WHAT IS PROSPECTING?

Getting started is often the hardest part of a job. People need all the energy they can muster, just for the starting. We're similar to cars: Only a small percentage of an engine's power is necessary to run a car, but all its power may be necessary to start it. Consider the following example:

Roger Bannister is a doctor in England. He'll probably never be remembered for his medical achievements, but most sports enthusiasts will recall his entry into the record books. As far as anyone knew, no one had ever run the mile in four minutes or less. Most people said it just couldn't be done.

Roger Bannister didn't believe the so-called experts. He began to plan the way he would do it, and then he trained. On May 6, 1954, he removed his obstacle by successfully running the first recorded four-minute mile. After this occurrence, funny things began to happen. Within the next four years, the four-minute mile was run by 46 runners. Roger Bannister had erased a mental barrier.

One of the basic elements of real estate sales is the systematic, planned approach to prospecting. All commissions earned begin with prospecting. Even the most experienced, successful and seasoned salesperson needs to prospect. If you diligently pursue as many approaches to prospecting as possible and use your skill to maximize your effectiveness when making the contact, your percentage of successful transactions will increase.

Prospecting Defined

The objective of prospecting is to work a systematic, planned approach to maximize your efforts in contacting potential customers in your listing bank.

You will prospect very heavily during the first two years of this business. Eventually, you will have developed a referral business from satisfied clients and you'll find yourself prospecting less than you used to.

Always, however, keep your prospecting techniques sharp. Time and experience have proven to the real estate industry that a "dry" time can eventually occur, bringing with it no active clients, no leads and nothing in escrow. In times such as these, even the most experienced and successful salesperson will have to start prospecting all over again.

FUTURE BUSINESS SOURCES

Keep your imagination working and your mind open to any sources for possible clients.

Referrals
- Business (merchants, professionals and so on)
- Friends, relatives
- Previous clients (from prior companies of employ)
- Service clubs and other organizations (civic, fraternal, etc.)
- Previous buyers, now sellers
- Previous buyers, wishing to buy more

Cold Contacts
- Reverse directory
- Newspaper ads (FSBOs)
- Newspaper notices (promotions, transfers and so on)
- Direct mailing campaigns
- Telephone prospecting
- Door-to-door contacts (just-sold method, just-listed method)
- For Sale signs on property

Expired Listings
- Your company's and others, and closed transaction files

WORK THE PERCENTAGES

Make the percentages work for you; use a variety of approaches to address the customer's needs and motivations.

When using the sources previously described, you will be working the percentages. You will be contacting many people, and out of these many contacts, only a small percentage will result in appointments. Historically, three appointments will be made of every 100 contacts. How you make the percentage work for you depends on your techniques and how well you perform them.

Remember these important factors when working the percentages:

- You must have the ability to fail part of the time.
- You can't get them all.
- Don't take *no* personally; it might be only a temporary no.
- Everyone has a fear of rejection; know this and expect to be rejected part of the time.

As an example of the last statement, consider the story of a boy born in Kentucky more than a century ago.

> This boy spent most of his youth working as a salesclerk in an Illinois store. Throughout his life, he probably didn't have more than a year of formal education. One day, he purchased a barrel of junk for 50 cents at an auction. In the whole barrel there wasn't anything of value except two books: law books.
>
> This young man read those books from cover to cover many times over. Sometimes, he would read in the evening in front of the bright fire of the fireplace. Sometimes, he would read by the early light of morning as it crept through the cracks of the walls of the log cabin in which he and his family resided. He read and read, preparing himself for that one day when his time would come.
>
> As he grew into manhood, sometimes he would travel as far as 50 miles on foot to obtain a book to read. He was paying the price to bring his planned goals into a reality.

Obviously by now, I'm sure you know I speak of Abraham Lincoln, the 16th president of the United States.

Because of his character, insight, courage and determination to overcome adversity, he endeared himself to millions of people over the world.

Let's look at Lincoln's list of rejections:

- He lost his job in 1832.
- He was defeated in his bid for the state legislature in 1832.
- His business failed in 1833.
- His sweetheart died in 1835.
- He had a nervous breakdown in 1836.

- He was defeated for Speaker of the House in 1838.
- He lost his bid for nomination to Congress in 1843.
- He was not renominated for vice president in 1856.
- He lost in his bid for the Senate in 1858.

He persisted, however, and finally won his big victory; he was elected president of the United States in 1860.

In working toward your goals, keep in mind what motivates customers:

- Taxes
- Depreciation
- High equity
- Changing area
- Home too small for growing family
- House too large; children moved out
- Desire to move up or down (status)
- Divorce
- Death in family

Your clients will have different motivations or needs; your job is to identify and *help address them*.

Remember, there are two reasons anyone would let you help solve his real estate problems:

1. The customer can't do it alone.
2. This is your chosen profession.

HOW TO CONTACT POTENTIAL CUSTOMERS

Your objective is to use as many approaches as possible that will be effective; to determine what approach to use in keeping with the prospect's motives; and to employ your skill to maximize the effectiveness of the contact.

To review these techniques, reread Chapters 1 and 2. Otherwise, it's assumed that you have set your goals, are using a daily planner, have toured property, are familiar with your marketing area, have an up-to-date mailing list, know how to use direct mailings, know how to use the telephone effectively and are versed on the services you're supposed to offer the client.

You must be consistent in your prospecting; therefore, you need to keep your name and that of your company before the client at all times. Think of the direct mail you've received; those that have come on a consistent basis are probably those to which you eventually respond. It's a matter of timing.

When your listing bank information is up-to-date, you should have an accurate mailing list from which to work. You should make at least 11 contacts a year in your listing bank through direct mail, telephone calls and door-knocking.

A suggested program might be as follows:

Action Step 1   Each day, five days a week, mail out ten direct mail pieces—50 a week.

Action Step 2   Make ten follow-up phone calls per day, five days a week.

Action Step 3   Knock on the doors of ten homes per day, five days a week.

Action Step 4   Follow up with the owners of these homes by mail.

Follow Up

Extend yourself one step beyond what the prospect might expect of you. Make the time to write personal responses to prospects who were helpful to you or interested in your services; use the telephone as another means of following up.

A biologist tells the story of how he watched an ant carrying a piece of straw that seemed a big burden to it: The ant came to a crack in the sidewalk that was too wide to cross. The ant stood for a time as though pondering over the situation. Then it put the straw across the crack and walked on it.

The lesson for everyone of us is this: Your burdens can be made into a bridge for new progress. All human progress has been made by people desiring to break records, overcome burdens, excel and meet challenges that have been thrown at them. They wanted to do things better and to do things that have never been done before. Stretch your mind and visualize yourself doing bigger things.

Anytime someone responds to you with a possible lead, indicates an interest in selling or knows someone who is, send a personal note of thanks for the time and whatever information you received. This is a rather unexpected action and would be considered one step beyond what the average salesperson would do. It also has a direct impact on what that person thinks of you.

SAMPLE NOTES

Dear

Just a note to thank you for referring _____
to me. You can be assured that I will do my best to help these
nice people and justify your confidence in me.

Sincerely yours,

_____
(signature)

Or

Dear Mr. and Mrs.

I certainly appreciate the opportunity to discuss your real
estate situation with you. You can be assured that when you
are ready to move, I will do my very best to find a good, qualified buyer and get you comfortably moved.
    If any questions arise, please feel free to call.

Cordially,

_____
(signature)

Use the telephone to contact any people you missed while door-to-door prospecting. Complete any information obtained on your client card.

Keep a complete record of all contacts you make in your listing bank; without organization, you take the chance of a sloppy hit-or-miss situation.

THE PONY EXPRESS IS ALIVE AND WELL— DIRECT MAIL CAMPAIGNS

As professional real estate salespeople, we have a great opportunity to light up the lives of our prospects. We can truly be of service and provide benefits to our clients. Consider the story of the old village lamplighter:

> Each evening, at dusk, the village lamplighter would gather his tools and make his way up the street, lighting the lamps as he went. The lamplighter would go to the first lamp pole, place his ladder, climb up the ladder and remove one of the panes of glass. Then he'd clean all of the glass, trim the wick and finally, after it was all ready, light the lamp.
>
> He would then climb down the ladder, pick it up along with his other tools and go on to the next lamp. Lamp by lamp, light by light, he would make his way up the street, shining, trimming and lighting. Soon he would disappear from sight, but you could always tell where he had been by the lights he had lit.

I'm sure you would like to sell in a way that you, too, could always tell where you've been, by the client's enjoying benefits from the services you have offered.

Direct mail solicitation is an extremely important part of your everyday prospecting activities. Send something that will benefit or be useful to the client. Do not use mail pieces to brag about your successes or even your company's.

Your objective is to keep your and your company's name before the prospective client. Sooner or later, one of your mailings will strike a responsive chord and the client will call or return a card requesting further information.

To be effective, you must be consistent and organized. Always enclose a response device, such as on postage-paid return card. Follow up the mailings with a phone call. When you get a reply, follow up right away.

Keep your mailing list updated, since properties transfer ownership. Be alert to new ideas that you can use in your mail program. Exchanging ideas with other salespeople and management can be helpful to all.

Many different types of mailers are available. Be aware of any client's reactions, so that you may stay effective.

Organize

Compile the mailing list from your listing bank. Your mailing list should consist of around 400 addresses. To compile your mailing list, make good use of reverse directories and assessors' books.

Organize each home in your listing bank on either a client card or 3" × 5" index card. If you are computerized, use a database or contact management program.

Develop a mailing program and work it into your daily planner. Consider

- what mailing pieces you're going to use.
- when you intend to mail them.
- what portion of your listing bank you're mailing to, if not to the entire listing bank.

One of your first mailings should include announcement cards with your business card.

Make notations on your client cards as to what pieces were sent to which home and when. You'll build a complete history of each home and the types of contacts they've received from you. Shortly, you'll contact these people by phone, and will need to know what contact you've had with them (see Chapter 4).

Build a variety of mailing pieces into your program. Prevent your prospective clients from becoming so accustomed to receiving the same items that they automatically throw them away before opening them.

Mail on a very consistent basis to be certain you are mailing to everyone and not contacting people sporadically. Keep your name before prospective clients, but don't deluge them to the point of being offensive.

Again, the need for you to be organized can never be overemphasized.

Mailers

There are many ways of using variety in your mailings. Here are a few:

- *Company brochures.* These alone offer many varieties.

- *Form letter or letter of solicitation.* A personal letter on the company letterhead from you, sent with any type of content: an offer of service or of a comparative market analysis of their home, or news of current real estate trends that affect their home's value.

- *Just sold or just listed cards.* These effective notices are used to keep your clients informed as to what is going on in their neighborhood.

- *Neighborhood newsletter.* This can be on company letterhead or take another form with news the prospective client would be interested in relating to neighborhood activities in schools, clubs, art shows or cultural events.

- *Neighborhood calendar.* At the end of each month, send out the following month's calendar with neighborhood activities marked on the day they'll occur. Personalize it with your name, picture, company name or whatever else you think might be important to the client.

ACTION COMMITMENTS

I have read the previous section and realize I must do the following:

TO DO	TARGET DATE OF COMPLETION	ACTION COMPLETED
1.		
2.		
3.		
4.		
5.		
6. Meet with sales manager.		

SOURCES OF LEADS

With your planned program in mind, the following sources are presented to you with suggestions on how to make the contact:

- Reverse directories
- Newspaper ads and For Sale/FSBO signs
- Newspaper notices
- Door-to-door, in-person contacts
- Expired listings

Reverse Directory   Your office has a telephone directory that is reversed; the address is first, name second. It is an excellent source to use for making up your mailing list in your listing bank.

From the reverse directory, you can use the information obtained through phone calls (see Chapter 4), direct mail, and door-to-door, in-person contacts.

Newspaper Ads and For Sale/FSBO Signs   When you notice a For Sale by Owner ad in the newspaper, it can be a good prospect for you. Also, you might come across a FSBO sign while driving through your listing bank. This can be a good source, too.

Regarding a newspaper ad, some analysis of how the ad is written can sometimes help you determine the following:

- Motive
- Urgency
- Professional seller

If the above questions can be answered from the ad, it can give you an approach to use when contacting the client.

▼ **ACTION RECALL**

For Sale By Owner Ad or Sign

Objective:

Make an appointment to see owners and give presentation.

Steps:

- Introduce yourself.

- Acknowledge the ad or sign.
- Ask about their interests.
- Compliment the home's exterior; ask to see interior.
- Look for motivation.
- Establish relationship.
- Get an appointment.

(For more information, reread Chapter 4.)

Suggested Language:

"Hello, This is _____ with Sunny Realty. How has the activity been on your ad?"

Or

"I couldn't help noticing your attractive ad in the paper today. How is the activity?"

Or

"I have some interesting market survey data you may like to look at. May I bring my comparative market analysis to you at 2 P.M. or would 4 P.M. be better?"

Local Newspapers Make it a habit to read your local newspapers. Then follow up with a short note.
Some suggestions:

- *To the president of the PTA*

    "May I say what I believe is in the mind of every parent in this community. . .thank you for your successful efforts on behalf of our school."
- *To the businessperson whose speech was reported*

    "The excerpts of your speech I saw in the paper were very interesting. Would it be possible for me to get a copy?"
- *To the parents of a newborn*

    "I would like to take this occasion to share your happiness on the birth of your (son) (daughter)."
- *To the person who was promoted*

    "I have heard several people express pleasure at your promotion. I would like to add my congratulations."
- *To the parents of a winner of scholastic honors*

"My pride and confidence in our young people are never stronger than they are when I hear of someone like your (son) (daughter)."

- *To the service club president*

"The entire community is indebted to you and your membership for spearheading the drive for funds for _____."

Door-to-Door, In-Person Contact   We have mentioned that it is vitally important to be consistent in your prospecting and to keep your name and your company before the client at all times. This is also true of keeping yourself visible on a consistent basis, where allowable, depending on the restrictions of your listing bank.

If you are able to, knock on every door in your listing bank; make yourself known to your clients. Everyone receives direct mail, but it helps a great deal to connect a face and personality to the mail they've received. It also establishes in their minds the visible fact that you are out there working, a fact that might impress them if they are thinking of selling and want to know what you would do for them.

Consider the human factor when working door-to-door: First, what initial reactions do you expect from potential customers? There will usually be a natural resistance. Then, consider your own natural reaction to the client's resistance. Usually, you will feel rejection, or foresee impending failure.

Remember, work the percentages; expect to fail part of the time. Don't take "no" personally. You're going to contact many people who will tell you, "no, not now," but some will say "yes."

Organize yourself before you even attempt to make contact. Create a route out of your 3" × 5" index cards, or use client cards in the order in which you'll travel. If you use a computer, print out the information you will need.

Action Step 1   Always look up comparables. Be familiar with any recent activity.

Action Step 2   Refer to the owner by name; always talk to the homeowner.

Action Step 3   If you come across a name that is not on your list, make a note of it and obtain the name from a neighbor.

Action Step 4 If a homeowner just bought, always ask if they have friends or relatives who may be considering a move into the area and if they know of anyone from where they've moved who's thinking of buying or selling.

Action Step 5 Make notes of any information obtained on the 3" × 5" cards.

The Approach

- Don't walk across lawns.
- Don't stand too close to the door.
- Always introduce yourself and your reason for calling.
- Always compliment the home if a compliment is due.
- **Important!! . . . Be confident in your manners!**

▼ **ACTION RECALL**

Door-to-Door Prospecting

Objective:

To locate potential sellers.

Steps:

- Introduce yourself, give your company name and your business card.
- Establish rapport.
- Inquire about potential sellers (neighbors).
- Ask if they have considered selling.
- If interested, ask to see the inside of their home.
- Get an appointment to meet spouse.
- Thank the person to whom you've been speaking.

Suggested Language:

"Good morning. I'm _____, with _____.
How are you this morning? I was just admiring your attractive front yard. This is my chosen area, and I have been making a survey to determine the market activity of the area. Would you know of any of your neighbors who might be thinking of selling?"
"Have you considered selling your home?"
In conversation, include the following:
"How long have you lived here?"

"Were you transferred in from out of state?"

"What are some of the things you like about this neighborhood?"

"By the way, when will you be thinking of selling?"

Always close the conversation with:

"Thank you. I'll be checking with you from time to time to see if I can be of any assistance should you have any questions about real estate. In the mean time, if you have any friends or relatives who might be thinking of buying or selling, I'm sure you'd want them to have reliable professional guidance, wouldn't you? Well, then, I'd like to leave three of my cards with you. I'd appreciate it if you'd give one to them. I'll be happy to help them in any way I can. Thank you again."

(If you receive a lead, go direct. If not, go on to next home.)

EXPIRED LISTINGS

Why does a listing expire? Studies conducted in various real estate markets clearly show that our inflationary trends leave most owners with inflated price conditions. If the owner's listing salesperson has not researched local, up-to-date market conditions and trends, the odds are increasingly in favor of an overpriced listing. The price was probably based on what a neighbor's home listed for, not what it actually sold for.

In short, homes sell for one or all of three basic reasons: emotion, price and terms.

The owners' resentment toward the salesperson after the listing has expired can be understood by analyzing the following statements:

"All you real estate people are alike. You get my listing and forget it. We never hear anything."

In this case, there was no follow up: no notes to let the owner know what the salesperson was doing, no phone calls, no response to an open house. No contact was made by the salesperson to let the owner know he or she was working.

"We're not interested in another broker; we'll sell it ourselves."

Since the owners didn't see the salesperson work, they feel they can do it themselves.

Knowing why a listing expired can help you understand the owners' attitudes at the time you contact them and can also help you determine how to counter objections and help sell the house.

▼ ACTION RECALL

Expired Listings

Objective:

To get appointment to meet spouse and make presentation.

Steps:

- Introduce yourself.
- Inquire about availability.
- Get inside the home.
- Look for the owner's motivation.
- Establish a relationship.
- Get an appointment.

Suggested Language:

"This is _____ of Sunny Realty. I noticed that you no longer have a sign up. Have you sold your home or is it still available?"

"Is a REALTOR® currently representing you in the sale of your home?"

If no

"How soon can you give possession?"

"What time may I see your home today?"

Or

"May I see your home this morning, or would this afternoon be better? "

"Do your plans include another attempt to sell your home now?"

"Do you have any ideas about why your home did not sell?"

"If you still want to sell your home, can you see any disadvantage in knowing two possible reasons it did not sell? I can explain it to you in about 15 minutes; would tonight at 7 P.M. be all right, or would 8 P.M. be better?"

Note: Remember, make your presentation in question form and not the average "do you want to list your home?"

Remember!! . . . *All commissions earned began with prospecting. All prospecting begins with a plan.*

ACTION COMMITMENTS

I have read the previous section and realize I must do the following:

TO DO	TARGET DATE OF COMPLETION	ACTION COMPLETED
1.		
2.		
3.		
4.		
5.		
6. Meet with sales manager.		

7 The Process of Listing

The essence of real estate brokerage is getting control of the right property, at the right price, at the right time. The organized and effective way to get control of property is by listing it.

The listing process helps you gain control of the seller through property and customer qualification, and by influencing the terms of the listing.

By energetically following the process set forth in this chapter, you will get control of property, thereby making a transaction happen.

After you have completed this chapter, you should be able to

- identify listing procedures.
- describe the process of listing.
- describe how to conduct the first listing meeting.
- list steps to take to prepare for the second meeting.
- describe how to conduct the second meeting so as to get the listing.
- proceed with servicing the listing in a manner that will satisfy the seller.

What exactly is involved in listing a property? The following will show you the progression of events leading up to a listing. It is important to know how to apply skills and resources in the systematic listing of a property.

Prospect list:	Prepare listing bank data, mailing lists, records of market activity, client cards; tour property; and research previous transaction files.
Prospect plan:	Prepare permanent card file by property; use daily planner to determine call priorities and call schedule; and use ACTION recalls for call strategies.
Obtain appointment:	Contact by telephone, personal letter, direct mail or door-to-door solicitation or other in-person contact.
First meeting with prospect:	Basically, this is a fact-gathering session; the purpose is to determine the seller's needs and wants; to see, measure and physically inspect the home; to begin qualifying; and to make a second appointment.
Prepare for second meeting:	Use this interval to evaluate the property, prepare your listing presentation, prepare a competitive market analysis (CMA) and recommend a listing price.
Second meeting:	This meeting serves two purposes: to get the listing and get it at the right price.
Service the listing:	Use every means to sell the listing, communicate to the seller all activities on behalf of the property and provide service after sale.

Since the first half of the listing process, prospecting for leads, has already been discussed, this chapter will cover the following:

- The first meeting with the potential client
- Preparing for the second meeting
- The second meeting
- Servicing the listing

THE FIRST MEETING

Your objective in conducting a two-visit listing appointment is to acquire the maximum amount of information, evaluate the property (by seeing the home in the daytime) and establish an early rapport for the evening appointment.

Depending on the type of contact, you may wish to set only one appointment with your prospect initially. As a condition of that appointment, ask to see the home in the daylight before the evening appointment.

If you make the initial contact as part of your door-to-door rounds, ask to see the home and then set up an evening appointment. If you make the initial contact by phone, make the evening appointment first, then ask whether either spouse would be at home to show you through during the day.

Before you leave for the first appointment, always take the time in the office to list comparables.

Once at the property, observe it from the curb and note the following:

- Immediate area (good/bad)
- Landscaping (good/bad)
- Paint and trim (good/bad)
- "Curb appeal" (first impression)

Be on time. The customer's first impression of you is lasting.

Greet the sellers. Give them your card. Explain the purpose of your two visits. Gain information (loan, taxes, insurance, title, condition, etc.). Inform the sellers of your competitive market analysis (CMA) and precondition them to your ability. Ask to view the property in the daytime. Start qualifying.

Tour the home with the sellers. Measure the rooms, inspect all features, and observe the overall condition and improvements. Note all items that will add or detract from value. Note from conversation schools, etc. Do not discuss price.

Thank the sellers and reconfirm the date and time of your evening appointment.

▼ **ACTION RECALL**

Qualifying the Seller

Objective: To determine the urgency and motivation of sellers.
Steps:

- If contact is made by the seller's call to the office, qualify on the telephone.
- Further determine motivation at first and second meetings.

Suggested Language: (Use questions as needed in conversation.)

"Are you being transferred or will you be looking for another home in town?"

"How soon do you have to move?"

"When we find the right buyers, how soon could they take possession?"

"Have you sold before? Have you used the services of a broker before?"

"Are you familiar with recent sales prices in the area?"

"Will you need all your money from this sale to purchase your next home?"

"How long have you lived in this home?"

"If the house does not sell before you leave, will your spouse remain?"

THE SECOND MEETING

Your objective in the second meeting is to review the owners' needs and their property; to prepare a listing package based on the maximum amount of comparable information available and your evaluation of the property itself; and to prepare a planned presentation.

Preparation

Answer the following questions about the owners' needs and their property.

- How long have they lived there?
- Where do each of the owners work?
- When, where and why are they moving?
- Why are they selling?
- How soon do they have to move? Also, determine as many facts as you can about the property. Present CMA and recommend a price (see Chapter 3). In doing so, you'll need to research comparables, including expired and For Sale comparables; if unfamiliar with them, try to go see them.

Once you have gathered all this information, you are ready to prepare a listing package, a portfolio for the owners, including documentation of your findings, your plan for selling their home and any other information they may be interested in. It should be prepared to project a professional image, and to be a document the owner will want to keep.

The listing package should include the following:

- A title page
- A personal letter to the clients
- Your marketing plan for their home
- Your evaluation of their property
- The CMA
- Your recommended price

It may also include the following:

- Samples of newspaper advertising
- Sample "Just Listed" cards, various brochures and other marketing materials
- Relocation information

Prepare a planned listing presentation—the vast majority of professional salespeople rehearse their plan beforehand. Review all the information in the listing package. Fill out the entire listing agreement except for price and terms.

Anticipate possible objections from seller and methods for countering them. Review the 11 steps of the presentation. (See "At the Second Meeting," following immediately.) Rehearse a net sheet; have one ready if needed.

At the Second Meeting

Get the listing and get it at the right price; know when to turn down the listing. Structure your presentation as follows:

Action Step 1   Get to know the sellers. Let them know your concern for their interests.

Action Step 2   Review home with the sellers. Let them know you know about their home. Acknowledge the improvements, time and thought that the sellers put into their home.

Action Step 3   Lead them to a table, preferably in a breakfast area. Take control.

Action Step 4   Pay a *sincere* compliment; they will see through a phony one.

Action Step 5   Sell yourself and your company through your marketing plan. Let the sellers know what you are going to do for them that surpasses the efforts of other salespeople. *Remember* . . . Don't make promises you don't intend to keep.

Use visual aids; show and tell them how you're going to do it. Share your ideas: mail-outs, advertising, brochures, signs, relocation, etc. Start to use assumptive selling: change from "You and I" to "we."

Action Step 6   Present CMA. Let it stand alone. Give the sellers time to look it over after you have explained how to read it.

Action Step 7   Close on price range. Ask the sellers to decide: "Based on competitive sales, it seems the buying public is paying between $_____ and $_____ for a home comparable to yours. At what price should we market your home?

The price range should be within 5 percent of other comparables.

Action Step 8   Discuss terms. Have a net sheet on hand, if needed.

Action Step 9   Complete the listing agreement.

Action Step 10   Close for approval. Say, "With your approval, we can begin marketing your home". . .Hand the decision-maker a pen for his or her signature. Never tell sellers to "sign here."

Action Step 11   Precondition the sellers. Inform them on upkeep and repair needs; let them know you will show them all offers; inform them about agent previews, keys and lock boxes; controlling house pets, and so on.

If you encounter any serious objections from the owners regarding the price, and you have made *every* effort to counter their objections, remember that you have a last-ditch option to bring them to a realistic price range, to educate them to what the market trend is: *You can turn down the listing*.

If you seriously believe the price they want will render the property unsalable, you have to decide whether it is worth spending your time on it. Don't forget: You have presented a marketing plan for their home; you are committed to doing everything you have said you would do if you agree to take the listing. Is it going to be a waste of your time? Make your decision.

You might find that if you decide against taking the listing at the price the owners want, and tactfully explain to them your reasons for not doing so, they will respect you more for it and change their minds. But do not use this as a closing tactic; it should only be a legitimate situation, not a tool to manipulate.

This option applies not to small differences in selling price, but to situations where there is a great spread, and when the clients are definite in their opinion. If you've presented all the comparative evidence, and they still refuse to agree, then the decision is yours.

SERVICING THE LISTING

Your objective is to use every means available to you to sell the listing, to communicate to the sellers all activity on their property and to service the listing after the sale.

First Week   In the first week of your listing, submit listing information to the local Board of REALTORS® to facilitate publication of the listing in the Multiple Listing Service and to your manager for advertising. Make your first presentation at the office sales meeting and encourage your office sales staff to preview the home.

Second Week   Conduct an open house for other agents, and advise sellers of their comments. Schedule a minimum of two public open houses per month.

Third Week   Make a second presentation at your office sales meeting, contact the sellers regarding your progress and send them copies of anything you mail out regarding the listing ("just listed" cards, open house invitations, ads if advertised, etc.).

Fourth Week   Check with local corporation personnel directors for incoming potential clients.

Fifth Week   Hold second open house for other brokers and advise sellers of their comments.

Sixth Week   Discuss listing progress with your manager; make a third presentation at your office sales meeting.

Seventh Week   Arrange a second showing for your office sales staff; advise sellers of their comments.

Eighth Week   Visit sellers for review of activity to date.

You will note that you have built into your planning regular communication with the sellers as to what you are doing to sell their home. They need to know what you are doing for them. Advise the sellers weekly as to

- reactions of potential buyers after all showings.
- activity at open houses—show them the guest book, inform them of reactions, etc.
- new listings in the area (know your competition).
- recent sales in the area.
- general market conditions.
- loan market.

Remember, since you represent the seller in all negotiations, you must present all offers.

After the Sale

Servicing the listing does not stop when the sellers have received an offer and the home is sold.

You must keep the sellers advised as to the progress of the transaction to the successful close of escrow. (In some areas of the country, this period is referred to as "under agreement.")

Hand-carry all documents when logistically possible. Keep a complete file and log of all documents and correspondence pertinent to the transaction for ready reference. All originals are to be kept in the office with the transaction file; you keep a duplicate.

LISTING CHECKLIST

Check "yes" or "no" for each answer.

Yes	No	
❏	❏	1. Develop your prospect list.
❏	❏	2. Set priorities and establish a prospecting plan.
❏	❏	3. Arrange your first meeting with prospective customers.
❏	❏	4. Before you leave the office, list all comparables.
❏	❏	5. As you arrive at the property, check to see if it has "curb appeal."
❏	❏	6. The first meeting has two major purposes: to establish you as an authority and to start your evaluation of the home.
❏	❏	7. In preparing for your second meeting, • Review the facts about the customers' needs and their property. • Conduct a CMA. • Prepare your listing package. • Prepare (and rehearse) your planned listing presentation.
❏	❏	8. The basic purpose of the second meeting is to get a listing on the property at the right price.
❏	❏	9. To impress the prospect with your ability, talk a great deal about the area, the pricing and the market time prior to a sale.
❏	❏	10. A comprehensive knowledge of all potentially competitive listings is an important part of your planned listing presentation.
❏	❏	11. Use visual aids whenever you can to aid in comprehension.
❏	❏	12. Try to educate the owners on specific sales prices in the area.
❏	❏	13. Always relate terms to asking prices.
❏	❏	14. In marketing your listing, select the several sales avenues that are most likely to be successful and direct your time and energy there.

ACTION COMMITMENTS

I have read the previous section and realize I must do the following:

TO DO	TARGET DATE OF COMPLETION	ACTION COMPLETED
1.		
2.		
3.		
4.		
5.		
6. Meet with sales manager.		

SAMPLE LISTING PACKAGE

Competitive Market Analysis

Prepared for:

Mr. and Mrs. Bob Seller
4912 N. Christiana
Sunny, Anywhere 00000

Prepared by: _____
(Your Name)

Date:

Name:

Street:

City, State:

Dear Mr. and Mrs. Seller:

In estimating the fair market value of your property, I have carefully considered all relevant factors. My analysis uses the same variables that a professional fee appraiser utilizes: a combination of current market conditions, square footage, location, property condition and features and comparable recent sales. Please bear in mind that my analysis is based on today's market, and that appreciation and the economy change.

Enclosed is a list of comparable properties in your neighborhood that have sold during the last years. While none of these homes are particularly similar to yours, they do provide a basic reference in a competitive market analysis. We have toured many homes in the area that currently or very recently have been on the market. We feel that your home will be competitive with other comparable homes listed at $_____, with a variable of plus or minus 5 percent. Frankly, there are no comparables with the specific extra lot addition. Even though this lot lends privacy and seclusion, it would be extremely costly to develop.

Beginning at $_____ to test the market would be my advice, followed by a periodic review to see if we are competitive. The price you ultimately will receive, of course, will depend on your motivation and the motivation of the buyer.

I am most anxious to represent you in the event you desire to market this most charming and attractive home.

Cordially,

_____
(Your Name)
Owner: _____
Address: _____
Assessor's parcel number: _____
Assessed value: _____
Taxes—1992–93: _____
Lot size: _____

The Seller home is located in a desirable neighborhood of well-maintained homes. English Tudor in style, the house is a two-level with stucco exterior, wood with trim and wrought iron gates across the entryway. The entry and dining room floors are Spanish tile. The sunken living room has a cathedral ceiling with exposed beams and planked hardwood flooring. The fireplace is made of used brick. The room is graced by a large bay window. Doorways are arched and the wood trim is in excellent condition.

Consisting of four bedrooms and two and one-half baths, the home is in excellent condition.

Some special features that should be noted are as follows:

1. Within the last five years, the home has had a new furnace and roof.
2. The home contains a central vacuum system.
   Continue your list with any other relevant features.
   Room Descriptions
   Entry:
   Living Room:
   Dining Room:
   Kitchen:
   Bedrooms:
   Bathrooms:
   Basement:
   Garage:
   Rear Yard:

General: The privacy and seclusion offered by the additional lot to the rear make this home very marketable if priced in a realistic and competitive manner.

A charming and unique home with very attractive grounds, which are well landscaped.

Etc., etc. . . .

Include your CMA in your listing package.

Reminder: Allow the potential sellers a sufficient amount of time to read the CMA and ask questions.

Since it may have been some time since you sold your previous home, I have listed normal seller's closing costs:

1. *Commission.* _____% of the selling price.
2. *Revenue stamps for the deed.* $_____ per $1,000 of the selling price.
3. *Structural pest control clearance.* Before a lending institution will provide a loan, they will require a licensed termite infestation and fungus inspection, among others.
4. *Prepayment penalty, if any.* Check with your lending institution.
5. *Pro rata share of taxes.* Depending on your impound account and the date of the close of escrow, you may have a credit.
6. *Reconveyance of deed from the lender.* $_____
7. *Fire insurance policy.* Credit, unless you are transferring it to another home purchase.
8. *Interest on existing loan(s).* Approximately $_____ month.
9. *Miscellaneous fees: drawing documents, recording and notary fees, etc., about $_____*
10. Other. . .

Presented by: _____
Your Name

Presentation of Offers. We represent your interest in all negotiations.

After-Sale* Service. Whenever possible, I shall do the following:

- Keep you advised as to the progress of the transaction to the successful close of escrow.
- Hand-carry all escrow documents when logistically possible.
- Keep a complete file of all documents pertinent to the transaction for ready reference.

*In some areas of the country, *after-sale* is referred to as *under agreement.*

Where Do the Buyers Come From?

Most homeowners believe that buyers for their home are obtained from the newspaper ads on their homes. Actually, less than 5 percent of the homes are sold directly from the ads. We would like to acquaint you with the various sources of buyers.

When your home is sold, I can inform you as to the source of your buyer. Buyers come from many different sources:

- Many of our best qualified buyers today are yesterday's sellers.
- Corporate transfers are a major source of highly motivated buyers.
- Some come from personal referrals to our salespeople.
- Advertising also draws buyers: television, radio, newspapers, brochures, bulletins, magazines and directories.
- Others are referred by For Sale signs on property, or through open houses.

8 How To Conduct an Open House

An open house is a vehicle not only for obtaining buyers, but for obtaining listings. This chapter will show you the sequence of events before, during and after holding an open house.

The open house is an excellent prospecting tool, because not all people who go through an open house are buyers. Many are looking because

- They are thinking of selling their home, but are investigating current values before they sell; obviously, this is a good listing prospect.
- They are neighbors who are comparing the home to theirs to see what their home is worth; this could be a possible selling lead.
- They are thinking of moving into the area before they sell their home; this could result in a possible sale and listing.

So, whatever the reason people attend open houses, keep your eye on your objective. If you let all of the little daily irritations and frustrations consume your energies, you will never achieve the big victory or the ultimate goal.

This chapter will cover the following topics with regard to open houses:

- Selecting the property
- Preparing yourself
- Preparing the owner
- Preparing the home
- Conducting the open house
- Closing the house

The chapter will conclude with an open house checklist.

SELECTING THE PROPERTY

When selecting a home for which an open house will bring you the desired flow of traffic and activity, keep the following in mind:

- The home should not be overpriced.
- It should not be on a main street.
- It should not be on a hard-to-find street.
- It should be in a much-desired area, based on current and past activity.
- It should be easy to locate by a prospective buyer.

PREPARING FOR THE OPEN HOUSE

Preparing Yourself

How will you prepare for the open house will determine how successful your efforts will be.

First, send open house invitations to neighbors within a few blocks of the home, not the entire listing bank. Do not mail to those neighbors living close by.

Second, hand-carry the invitations to the near neighbors. There are very definite advantages to doing this:

- A great number of homes are sold to friends of the neighbors.
- This face-to-face meeting provides you an opportunity to meet the neighbors on a different basis from the usual cold call.
- Most neighbors would love to see a home close to theirs. They are curious because it influences the value of their own home. Now that they have your invitation, they are free to visit it.
- By seeing you hand-carry the invitations to the neighbors and conducting the open house, the neighbors get to see how you work. They just might be thinking of selling in the near future; this way, they get to see what you can do for them.

Then inspect all listings in the immediate area. You might meet a potential buyer during the open house who likes the neighborhood, but whose needs the house you're holding open doesn't quite meet. If you know of available listings, you can direct the buyer to another, more appropriate property.

Preparing the Sellers

Be certain to inform the sellers of the purpose of the open house. Show them the invitations and tell them what you have done with the cards. Tell them you will let them know the responses of the lookers, and ask them to do the following:

- Plan to be away from the home during open house hours and for some time before to allow you to prepare the home. Most people feel they can't really look at the home or talk about it freely when the owner is present.
- Arrange to have pets away from home during the open house.
- Be certain owners' valuables, such as jewelry or items of sentimental value, are put away securely.
- Be certain the home is neat.
- Be certain that all toilets are flushed.
- Be certain the yardwork is done.
- Ask their permission for any of the items you think necessary from the following list.

Preparing the Property

1. Pick up newspapers, etc.

2. Arrange patio furniture. Be sure hoses are out of the walkways and driveways.

3. Close the garage door.

4. Open as many drapes as possible unless a window reveals something unattractive.

5. Turn on lights where needed: in dark areas, hallways, small rooms, etc.

6. Wash down the driveway; it looks better wet. If there is snow, be certain the seller has it plowed.

7. Turn on sprinklers briefly; shrubs look more attractive when damp.

8. A fire in the fireplace adds warmth, unless air-conditioning is lacking in the summer season. (Get permission from sellers.)

9. Baking aroma in a home is an excellent sales tool. You can create this without actually baking anything. Put about one teaspoon of vanilla in a bowl-shaped piece of foil. Keep foil open at top and place in the oven at about 275°F. Clear this with the sellers.

10. Have copies of the listing for the guests and fellow brokers.

11. Have a guest book and sign the first two lines yourself; no one likes to be the first to sign the book. This is another good way to add prospects to your mailing list.

12. Have a supply of business cards ready.

13. Serve coffee and cookies (with permission of seller). Hint: Be certain the coffee is really Hot! The guests will linger longer.

14. Tune stereo to a good FM station; leave volume low. You want to create only background music.

15. Never turn on the television and never bring reading material that's unrelated to real estate.

16. Place open house signs to obtain maximum visibility. Don't violate local ordinances. If using the lawns of the neighbors in the area, always ask permission first; leave a business card with them and thank them. After the open house, when retrieving the signs, inform these neighbors of your successful open house and thank them again for their assistance.

17. Send a thank-you note to the neighbors who had allowed you to place your signs. They are an excellent source for sellers in the future.

DURING THE OPEN HOUSE

Leave the front door open or ajar. That way, people feel invited. Greet people at the door, then step out of the way. Let people look at their leisure, but keep them in view and ask qualifying questions (see Chapter 10).

CLOSING THE HOUSE

1. Turn off lights.
2. Close the drapes.
3. Clean the refreshment area.
4. Put out the fire in the fireplace.
5. Turn off the oven.
6. Collect the copies of the listing and the guest book.
7. Lock up.
8. Leave a thank-you note for the sellers.

Remember: Always send thank-you notes to those who dropped in.

▼ ACTION RECALL

Open House Clients

Objective:

To get an appointment to show homes or list visitors' existing home.

Steps:

• Greet visitor, introduce yourself, give each client your card and record name, address and phone.

• Show home to visitor.

• While showing, ask qualifying questions.

- Explain benefits of working with you.
- Arouse interest.
- Obtain appointment.
- Follow up with thank-you note.
- Follow up with phone call.

Suggested Language:

"How long have you been looking for a home?"

"Would you like to live in this home?"

"Do you own a home or are you renting?"

"How many are in your family?"

"How soon would you like to be in a new home?"

"If this is not the right home for you, I have some others I think would interest you. Could we get together to look at some tomorrow at 1 P.M., or would 4 P.M. be better?"

OPEN HOUSE CHECKLIST

Check "yes" or "no" for each answer.

I. Approach

Yes   **No**

☐   ☐   • Was your appearance neat and professional?

☐   ☐   • Did you greet visitors in a warm and friendly way?

☐   ☐   • Did you make them feel welcome?

II. Qualifying

Yes   **No**

☐   ☐   • Did you ask three or more qualifying questions (needs, wants, how long looking, timing, ability to purchase, etc.)?

      • Did you attempt to determine

☐   ☐   • present residence?

Yes	No	
❏	❏	• type of employment?
❏	❏	• family requirements?

III. Demonstration

Yes	No	
		• Did you discuss the benefits of
❏	❏	• community?
❏	❏	• recreation in area?
❏	❏	• schools?
❏	❏	• shopping?
❏	❏	• employment in area?
❏	❏	• quality of neighborhood residents?
❏	❏	• pride of ownership?
❏	❏	• Did you attempt to sell the benefits of the home:
❏	❏	• Features
❏	❏	• Quality
❏	❏	• Condition
❏	❏	• Style
❏	❏	• Financing
❏	❏	• Price

IV. Closing

Yes   No

☐   ☐   • Did you take control from the beginning and maintain it?

☐   ☐   • Did you answer questions and then ask qualifying questions?

☐   ☐   • Did you attempt to overcome objections?

☐   ☐   • Did you ask the visitor's name and address?

☐   ☐   • Did you ask the visitors if they wanted the home?

☐   ☐   • If they didn't want the home, did you ask for an appointment to show other property?

V. Presentation

Yes   No

☐   ☐   • Did you have a planned presentation?

☐   ☐   • Did you allow flexibility in your presentation to meet each individual situation?

☐   ☐   • Did you conduct a tour of the home and demonstrate it, or did you leave the clients on their own?

VI. Conclusion

Yes   No

☐   ☐   • Do you feel you conducted an organized presentation?

☐   ☐   • Did you attempt to establish a rapport with the clients?

☐   ☐   • If you were a client, would you buy from you?

ACTION COMMITMENTS

I have read the previous section and realize I must do the following:

TO DO	TARGET DATE OF COMPLETION	ACTION COMPLETED
1.		
2.		
3.		
4.		
5.		
6. Meet with sales manager.		

9 How To Write Effective Ads

The words *real estate* once called to mind the corner lot for sale, a house about to change owners or an apartment to let.

In today's complex real estate market, these same two words cover a multitude of living and investment possibilities that require specialized knowledge and a diversified advertising approach.

The real estate industry historically has been a heavy user of newspaper advertising. Sometimes these ads are created by real estate salespeople without the benefit of professional advertising assistance. With this in mind, we offer some suggestions for effective ad writing in today's market.

Writing effective ads involves specific, learnable skills. Your objective is to learn the techniques you must know to get the most out of your ads and to compete successfully with the ads of other agents and brokers.

THE BASICS

Available Tools

Many advertising aids and tools are close at hand to assist you in writing better copy. Don't hesitate to borrow ideas from other ad writers. Read the classified sections of your newspapers for headline ideas, catchy words and phrases. Brochures from new home tracts can have a wealth of ideas. Use Roget's Thesaurus—a book of synonyms, colloquialisms and special expressions; also useful is Rodale's *The Word Finder,* a book that produces an augmentative word—one to embellish and add to an idea.

The Nuts and Bolts

The major objective is a visually appealing ad with good descriptive copy that makes the same points you would if you were face-to-face with the reader. Once you collect all your facts, you're ready to start.

1. *Start with the headline.* The headline should dominate the ad and highlight the property's single most salable feature: location, view, price, emotional appeal, architecture, condition or size. In captioning your ad, be bold, dramatic and original.

2. *Make the body copy easy to read.* Give specific details, concisely: the number and kind of rooms, age of house, "extras," aesthetic features, neighborhood, schools, transportation, outdoor and recreational areas and terms. Appealing adjectives and colorful word pictures can provide the "sizzle."

3. *Create a "clincher."* This phrase will stimulate the reader to do something positive, such as call your office, drop by to see the property or attend an open house.

4. *Identify yourself immediately.* Provide readers with easy-to-spot phone number, address, office hours or even directions to your office or to the property advertised.

5. *Use display type.* Larger "display" type will make your ad stand out on the page. It helps create a specific image, such as stability, forward-looking design, luxury offerings, ocean-view property, etc.

6. *Use visuals.* Provide the best visual possible, such as a photo or illustration, for display ads. Put it together. Indicate how

all the elements (headline, copy, clincher, identification and graphics) will go together. Give each element of your ad some "elbow room." Let the headline stand apart from the rest of the copy. If you list many separate properties or different services, give each one a little white space to make it seem important enough to stand alone.

7. *Personalize when possible.* Tell convenience to which school and what shopping center. Identify a brand name appliance (for example, a GE refrigerator/stove). Use the salesperson's name.

8. ***Be Truthful.***

9. *Place ads early enough for proofs to be submitted.* That way, you will have time for any last-minute changes or corrections.

10. *Make good use of the 12 "most persuasive" words in the English language:* Save, Need, Safety, Discovery, Money, Results, Easy, Proven, You, Health, Love and Guarantee. Always try to use a variety of these in all your ads.

The Newspaper Advertising Bureau recently released survey results stating that people planning to move within a year have one life-style element as a primary deciding factor. The most popular ones are: spaciousness, a showplace, safe neighborhood, ease of commuting, good place for children, privacy, solid comfort, a place to swim and keep fit, easy maintenance, lots of conveniences nearby, push button living (inside is most important) and natural surroundings (outside is most important).

People want to know a lot about the home they will buy. Putting as many facts into the ad as possible will help the ad attract the right buyer—the one who is most interested and ready to buy that particular home.

According to the newspaper advertising bureau's survey results, your readers are looking for the following:

District, neighborhood, area, etc.	82.4%
Price, terms, down payment	72.8%
Number of bedrooms	66.1%
Condition of the home and lot	63.3%
Location of schools and shopping	56.0%
Location of property	44.8%
Type of heating	43.2%
Kitchen facts	42.7%
Recreation room	42.3%

Garage (room for one or two cars)	39.8%
Possession date	28.3%
View (if there is one)	24.4%
Landscaping	23.5%

HEADLINES

The job of the headline is to get attention. Headlines can do this in a number of ways. Try them all!!

- With intrigue in personal or even poetic ways
- By offering something unique
- By being funny
- By being timely
- By catching the reader's eye because of a good layout
- By painting a vivid word picture

Some Are Clever

- Kiss Your Landlord Goodbye! And Say Hello To. . .
- Topless. . .
- Weed It and Reap. . .
- Help Stamp Out Rent. . .
- Fixer with a Future. . .
- You're Not Buying a Lemon, but a Peach. . .
- These Apartments Are for the Birds and the Bees and for You . . .
- Erotica. . .

Some Are Timely

- Be My Valentine. . .
- A Grand New Year. . .
- School's Out. . .
- Buy a Chimney for Santa and One for You, Too. . .

Some Are Picturesque

- Modern Doll House. . .
- Apple-Pie Condition. . .

- Bachelor in Paradise. . .
- Wagon Wheel Charm. . .
- Top o' Hill. . .

Some Offer a Bargain

- Fantastic Buy. . .
- Help. . .
- Beat Inflation. . .
- Champagne Taste, Beer Income. . .
- Peace of Mind. . .

Some Are Eye-Catching

- View! Pool!
- A Buy!
- Terrific Value. . .
- Reach for the Moon. . .
- Get Away from It All...

Some Are Intriguing

- You're Holding Up a Wedding!!!
- Cleopatra's Canoe. . .
- Let Me Seduce You. . .
- Cinderella. . .
- Old King Cole. . .
- Red Riding Hood. . .
- Batman and Robin. . .

Don'ts

Do not rely on a headline that teases or bullies. The reader may not be in the mood for either.

Do not use vague generalities, worn-out phrases or too many superlatives.

Do not create a word picture that leaves a credibility gap once the prospect sees the "quaint castle" is really a "crumbling cottage."

Do not use too many abbreviations so that the ad looks more like a puzzle than an invitation to buy or rent.

Do not feel you have to use up every quarter-inch of available space with art or copy. White space attracts attention.

Do not incorporate too many conflicting type faces and sizes.

AIDA—Four Basic Principles of Good Advertising

1. *Attention*. Your headline should attract specific prospects.
2. *Interest*. Expand on the headline, offer a benefit and get the reader to read the rest of the ad.
3. *Desire*. With good descriptive copy, make the reader want what you have to sell.
4. *Action*. Ask for it! Make it easy for the reader to respond.

Remember, you're selling a way of life, not just a place to live. Once you're well acquainted with the property, think about what it has to offer the different members of a family, a person living alone or someone who wants to use it as a business investment. Then, write the ad.

Sample Headlines

Family Size and Country
   Style for the Choosy Family
Where Family Fun Begins
Have a Full-Size House?
King-Size Family Home
Bright as the Morning Sun
Need More Elbow Room?
Raising a Family?
Sunshiny Kitchen
A New Kind of Home
A Place for Everything
All the Work's Done
Fresh as Spring
Spic and Span Inside and Out
Like To Fix Up an Old House?
A Garden Spot
A World of Living
Move in Today
Ideal Opportunity
Last Chance
Opportunity Is Knocking!!
Look No Further!

Move Fast on This
   Outstanding Buy
Now or Never
Once in a Blue Moon
Rare Opportunity
Opportunity Knocks Again
Opportunity Knocks Once!
This One Won't Wait
Owner Packing—Quick
   Possession
A Family Delight
Take Advantage—The Time
   To Buy Is Now!
Conversation Piece
Tomorrow May Be Too Late
To Settle Estate
Exceptionally Smart
Big Squeeze?
Cheerful Atmosphere
Peak of Happiness
Designed for Happy Living
Dream No More
Artistic!

For the House Gourmet
Great for Living
High on a Hill
Key to Happiness
Pretty as a Picture
Look What We Found
Authentic Early American
Better Take a Look
Flower Gardener's Delight
Especially for You
Halfway to Heaven
Tall Trees and Smooth Lawns
Honeymoon Special
Instantly Appealing
A Little Mansion
Lots of Trees
Nestled among Giant Trees
Have Your Own Orchard
Old World Charm
Rambling Ranch
Plenty of Elbow Room
Too Good to Last
Want To Be Envied?
Rich in Detail
A Rare Find
Architectural Masterpiece
White Colonial Arches
  Border the Property
Here's One for the Books
Hacienda Living
The Answer to Your Dreams
Unusual Amount of Living
Large Bright Rooms
The World at Your Feet
Space Throughout
You Will Always Be Glad
Everything in Apple-Pie
  Order
Little Things That Count
Garden-View Dining
Flawless French Provincial
Atmospheric Old Home, All
  "Copper Kettle" Style

Trip to Heaven
New Inside Kitchen
Truly Delightful
You'll Fall in Love with
  Island Kitchen
Want Space? Here It Is
Dramatic Sunken Living
  Room
Dramatic Two-Story Foyer
Study Alcove
Colorful Powder Room
Full-Length Sliding Glass
Lovely, Spacious
  Farm-Style_____
A Kitchen Every Mother Will
  Love
Doors Lead to
  Adjoining_____
Kitchen Love
A Warm, Friendly Fireplace
Endless Cupboard Space
Handy Sewing Room
Glamorous Parquet Floors
Club Room for the Kids
Built-in Workshop
A Distinctive Home Planned
  for Gracious Living
Impressive Vaulted Ceilings
Inspiring View
Massive Stone Fireplace
A Smart Split-Level
Spectacular Hanging Fixture
Spanish Colonial Red Tile
  Roof
A Lavish Home Steeped in
  New Orleans French Touch
A Quaint Two-Story English
  Cottage
Quiet Luxury with Iron
  Grillwork and Provincial
  Styling
Authentic Pennsylvania
  Dutch Farmhouse

Out of the Ordinary

Handsome Red Brick, White

Appealing French Provincial
Balcony

Prestige English Tudor

Pillar Wrought Iron Balcony

Cozy as Only True Cape Cod

A Cape Cod Setting

Breezeway Can Be Easily
Enclosed

Snow White Cape Cod

A Flagstone Patio

Homey New England Touches

Summer House

Mellow Old Brick Colonial

Provincial

Marvelous Patio and
Barbecue with Pillared
Porch

Stunning Departure from the
Ordinary

Loads of Extras, Too

For Family Breakfast or
Dinner Party You'll Enjoy
This Big Patio

Delightful Swimming Pool

Sheltered Cocktail Patio with
Cabanas

Tree-Shaded Patio

A Lovely Terrace Under
Stately Trees

Horse Lover's Delight

Champion's Training Ground

A Friendly Home for
Gracious Living and
Entertaining

Practice Your Putting

Quaint Country Place to Fix
Up

Swimming Pool and Bath
House

Circular Drive Sweeps to
Your Resort Luxury in
Your Own Rolling Acre Lot

On a Quiet Street

Early American Farmhouse

A Storybook Home

Ivy-Covered Brick

A Do-It-Yourself Home

White Fence with a Swinging
Garden Gate

Setting with Panoramic View

Penthouse in the Sky

Writer's Retreat

Nestled on Lovely Site
Overlooking Stream

Big Enough for a Tennis
Court

Bordered Acre Lot

Scenic Rolling Countryside

On a Winding Lane

Scenic Views

Manicured Garden

Inspiring View of Lovely
Countryside

Delightful Little Stream

Swim Year-Round

In-Town Convenience with
Backyard Country Setting

Trim White Fence

Tennis Anyone?

Bowling on the Green

Count Every Star

Playing Fields

A Child's Paradise

No Need for Two Cars in
This Handy Location

A Private Kingdom

Just a Hop, Skip and a Jump

Don't Buy This Home

Stately English

Breathtaking View

"Do It Yourself"

Dreamy View Hideaway

Pocket Rancho
Unusual But Terrific
Country Club Jewel
Bit of Switzerland
Dream House
Dramatically Situated
Your Own Park
Designed for Secluded Living
Mountain Eyrie in Town
Like an Eagle
Your Own Private Road
Very Private and Lovely on
  Picturesque Wooded Lot
Artfully Landscaped
Large, Secluded Wooded Lot
Neighbors *Do* Count
At the End of a Country Road
Peaceful Neighborhood
Well-Established
Like a Country Village
Neighborhood
Think Size, Be Wise
Expanse, Not Expense!
Summer Necessity
An Orange Grove
The Entertainer
Rewarding Life
Reflect in the Pool
Space Available
Nothing Left Out
Join the Fun
Starting Point
Come Where It's Cool
Pool 'n Patio
No Wimbledon, but You Can
  Play Badminton in the
  Backyard
A Little Cash, and Carry Her
  Over the Threshold
Serenity
Stirs the Imagination
House Pinching You?
A Private Kingdom

The Country Gentleman
The Possible Dream
Don't Simmer This Summer
The Life Savers
Mom's Home at Dad's Price
Blaze of City Light
A "Welcome" Home
Superb
Prestige-Minded?
Country Club Area
Prestigious Area
For Busy Parents
Star's Former Home
Period Piece
Let the Rest of the World
  Go By
Inspired by Frank Lloyd
  Wright
It's All in a Day's Play!
Are You a Nature Lover?
Not Fancy—Just Homey
Built for a Heap of Living
Try This for Sighs
Heat Relief
The View Goes on and on
We Hate To Rave, But
Plush as a Palace
Move-in-Able
Kingdom for Horses
T-Bone Value—Hamburger
  Price
Eye Appeal, Heart Appeal
Warm as Toast
Have Happy Children
AWOL—A World of Living
Retreat from the Heat
Careful, It's Loaded
Let's Have a Cookout
Neat and Complete
A Crackling Fire
SOS Means "Sold on Sight"
Do You Have a Wait Problem?
Let the Sun Shine In

Ever Steal a House?	This May Shock You
The Busy Man's Haven	Create a New Life
Cooped Up?	Prettied up! Priced Down!
Enchantment for Sale	Happiness Is. . .
Splash Party	Palace for a Pittance!
A Home Is a Savings Account	Hate To Paint?
Beauty and the Beast	Often Sought, Seldom Found
Grand Ole Shade Trees	Modern Doll House
Weed It and Reap	Instantly Appealing
Million-Dollar View	Keepsake of Yesteryear

DESCRIPTIONS

Property Features

Dining Room

- Enjoy sophisticated entertaining in formal dining room.
- Casual dining area off living room for mealtime relaxation.
- Enormous old-fashioned dining room perfect for large family get-togethers.
- Adds a note of elegance to everyday dining.
- Step-saving dining area separated by a food bar from kitchen.
- Sunny informality is the keynote of this fresh dining room.
- Dining room that invites lingering over that second cup.
- Meals served in this bright, friendly dining room are extra special.
- Family meals are special occasions in this dining room.
- Room seasoned for casual family dining or elegant entertaining.

Kitchen

- So complete and well planned—an inspiration to any cook.
- Step-saving, modern electric—a pleasure to cook in.
- Family-size kitchen big enough to really move around in.
- Soup or soufflé, cooking isn't dull or routine in this new beauty.
- Goodbye dishpan hands—built-in dishwasher does the job.
- Cook to your heart's delight in this spacious ultramodern kitchen.
- Time-saving appliances built into this work-saving kitchen.

- A beautifully designed kitchen, with cabinets and electric stove where they should be.

Architecture

- Rambling ranch-style home "out in the country."
- Contemporary ranch style invites casual enjoyment.
- An old home, thoughtfully and perfectly restored.
- Traditional in spirit and appearance, but modern in convenience.
- Beautifully built around garden-patio area for a Spanish feeling.
- Easy upkeep in this contemporary slump block home.

Outdoor Living

- Everyday is a vacation with a pool and patio pretty as this.
- The cure for weekday traffic pains . . . relax by your own pool.
- Backyard barbecue offers pleasant family get-togethers.
- A sun shrine for the whole family.
- Lots of shade for summer comfort.
- A huge backyard where you'll wish you could linger longer.
- Healthier, happier summers for the whole family with this pool.

Family Room

- A jolly sort of recreation room with an open fireplace.
- Practical family room saves wear and tear on home . . . and nerves.
- Your teenagers will love this secluded room for homework or parties.
- A family room of unusual proportion, utility and charm.
- Practically decorated family room that's serviceable and suitable to any occasion.
- Hobbyists love this hide-away room.
- Spicily decorated fun-room, with built-in bar.
- Cozy, informal center for the family's hobbies.
- Family room that's relaxation headquarters for the family.

Bedroom

- Secluded wing separates master bedroom and bath from living areas.
- Luxurious master bedroom accommodates the most lavish furnishings.
- A boy and his dog will love bunking in this rugged paneled bedroom.
- Quiet, airy bedrooms that induce restful slumber.
- Storybook nursery for littlest tot.
- No dodging furniture—there's loads of room in this bedroom.
- Bedrooms are small, but there are (number) of them!
- Waterproof walls in kid's rooms resist enemy attacks!
- Bedrooms owe their charm to carefully chosen wallpaper.

Bathrooms

- Splash-proof, all-tile bath makes bathing fun instead of a chore for the kids.
- Huge, dramatically decorated master bath has enclosed shower.
- Immaculate large bath with lots of storage space.
- Luxury bathroom includes two handy sinks to save morning traffic tie-ups.
- Waterproof wallpaper gives design and character to the unique bath.
- Splash-proof enclosure for the child who gives the dog a bath.
- Two handy sinks for the morning march of the toothbrush brigade.
- Roman luxury with this beautiful sunken bathtub.

Fireplace

- Conversations grow warmer in front of the crackling wood fire.
- Big brick fireplace is center of family room life.
- Surround this warm fireplace with your happy family.
- Old brick fireplace just like "Grandma's in the country."
- Spend happier holidays at your own cheery fireplace.
- Rustic fireplace for Early American lovers.
- Classic brick fireplace the whole family will cherish.

Living Room

- Charming, warm paneled room reflects your hospitality.
- Express your individuality in this dramatic sunken living room.
- No hemmed-in feeling in this large living room.
- Majestic, beamed cathedral ceiling in living room.
- A living room big enough for all your family to really live in.
- A great place for guests and cozy enough for two.
- Large living room divided dramatically by a change of floor levels.
- A living room ready, willing and able to live up to its name.
- The great outdoors in the great indoors through the compliments of large picture windows.

Utility or Mud Room

- No trackin' and sloppin'! Handy carport leads to mud room.
- Gleaming utility room is just off kitchen for convenience.
- Handy utility room with ample cupboard space.
- Planned storage cupboards and built-in laundry makes the utility room practical work center.
- Big utility room fills storage needs, doubles as home laundry.
- Finished utility room wired for laundry facilities and home freezer.
- Well-planned utility room makes wash day almost fun.

Garage/Carport

- Weather protector carport for (number) cars.
- Just a touch of your finger and automatic overhead doors open.
- Neatly arranged storage in this easy-to-clean garage.
- Spacious garage has workbench already built in.
- Finish garage interior . . . easy to convert into additional rooms.
- Carport entrance keeps you and your car shaded on those hot days.

Air Control

- Step into cool, clean air-conditioned living.
- Pick your own atmosphere and temperature. Home centrally climatized by (name).

- Beat the heat this summer! Move into this totally air-conditioned home.
- Efficient room air-conditioning cools you in seconds.
- Seal out sun and dust. Secure cool, clean living with (brand) refrigeration in this home.
- Comfort-assuring refrigeration lets you pick the temperature.
- Goodbye dust and pollen with centrally filtered air-conditioning.
- "Set and forget" year-round temperature control.

Location

- Safe walking to nearby school and neighborhood stores.
- Prosperous section where each home reflects pride of ownership.
- Privacy, yet only a few minutes from shopping.
- Handy to neighborhood stores where you're treated like a neighbor.
- A vital young family area with lots of neighborhood fun.
- Where everyone wants to live—but few have the chance.
- Schools for tots through teens conveniently located.
- Out in the country, where everything is fine.
- In surroundings you'll long to get home to.
- Neat homes and yards reflect community spirit.
- For the city boy, convenient to everything!
- Some of the greatest neighbors you'll ever meet, with shopping centers nearby.
- Ideal location—only a stroll to schools, shops, transportation.

Action Phrases

- Happy living starts here for your family. Hurry!
- If you've missed exceptional buys before, call this minute.
- Last time we offered one like this, it sold the first day, so hurry!
- If you've waited for an exceptional value, this is it! Call right now!
- Be safe today. Don't be sorry tomorrow you missed this terrific home buy.
- Don't be sorry next year—this year, it's going for only $_____.
- He who hesitates will find Sold on the door!
- There will always be tomorrow, but we can't guarantee this home will still be available then.

Houses for Sale

Ad Copy Essentials

Location	Landscaping
Construction	Possession date
Bathrooms	Distance to school, stores
Name, address, phone	Other rooms
Price, terms, down payment	Condition
Extras included (carpet, drapes)	Heating, plumbing
	Fireplaces(s)
Number of bedrooms	Garage
Architectural style	Reason for sale
Kitchen	

Key Descriptive Words and Phrases

Accessible	Enchanting	Innovation	Serene
Appealing	Endearing	Inspiring	Sparkling
Artistic	Endorsed	Inviting	Sturdy
Authentic	Endowed	Jewel-like	Substantial
Brilliant	Enduring	Lavish	Tempting
Becoming	Engaging	Lustrous	Thrilling
Captivating	Enticing	Luxurious	Traditional
Chic	Fascinating	Magic	Treasure
Convincing	Fashionable	Massive	Unblemished
Cherished	Flawless	Masculine	Unique
Classic	Friendly	Matchless	Unrivaled
Delicate	Genuine	Meticulous	Unsurpassed
Delightful	Gleaming	Novel	Vast
Dignified	Graceful	New	Velvety
Distinctive	Gratifying	Pace-Setting	Vibrant
Distinguished	Harmonious	Picturesque	Wholesome
Durable	Impeccable	Refreshing	Winning
Dramatic	Impervious	Refined	Youthful
Exquisite	Imposing	Satisfying	Zestful
Elite	Ingenious	Sensational	
Eminent	Immaculate	Sensible	

Condominium and Townhouse Living

Ad Copy Essentials

Location	Number of	Other rooms
Construction	bedrooms	Age
Condition	Architectural style	Kitchen
Heating, plumbing	Bathrooms	Levels
Fireplace(s)	Maintenance	Possession date
Garage	Price, terms, down	Distance to school,
Reason for sale	payment	stores,
Name, address,	Extras included	transportation
phone	(carpet, drapes)	

Key Descriptive Words and Phrases

Balcony view	Exciting 18-hole	Lighted tennis
Refreshing	golf course	court
swimming pool	Clubhouse facilities	Landscaped
Children's pool	Adult pool and	grounds
and play area	play area	24-hour security
Exercise rooms	Guest parking	Boat, trailer and
Seclusion	Immediate	camper storage
Maintenance-free	occupancy	Men's and
living	No more mowing	women's saunas
Magnificent	the yard	Private garage
courtyard	Private front and	Billiard room
Secluded privacy	rear entrances	
in condo		

Suburban Property

Ad Copy Essentials

Location (Be	Size of lot or	Roads and public
Specific)	acreage	transportation
Number of rooms	Distance from town	Price and terms
Landscaping and	Trees and view	Other buildings
trees	Garage	Room for livestock
School bus service	City utilities	Reason for selling
Heating	How and when to	
Garden, fruit trees	see	
Name, address,	Style and	
phone	construction	

Key Descriptive Words and Phrases

Raise your own vegetables

Raise your children on fresh air and fresh vegetables

Cut your property tax by one third

Abundance of shade trees

One small tractor and you're a farmer on this "farmette"

Completely fenced

Have fresh eggs every day

Great for green thumb artists

Only 15 easy minutes from downtown

No air-conditioning needed here

Ten degrees cooler in the summer

Wholesome refreshing

Yard big enough for a ball field

City convenience— country quiet

Build your own putting green

Sweeping view of green fields

Give your children room to run

Good roads all the way

Your city friends will envy you when they see it

Lots and Acreage

Ad Copy Essentials

Usage	Size	Access and roads
Residential development	Natural characteristics	Zoning (if any)
Industrial	Soil	Name, address, phone
Crop planting	Trees	Price and terms
Single residence	Terrain	
Location	Utilities available	

Key Descriptive Words and Phrases

Located in the path of progress

Prized location

The perfect lot for your lovely new home

Investor's dream

Low tax area

Fast growing section of city

Utilities in and paid for

Distinctive location

Parklike setting

Ripe for development

Only ___ minutes from _____

Accessible location

Matchless location

Unblemished natural beauty

Farms and Farmland

Ad Copy Essentials

Number of acres	Name, address, phone	Availability
Kind of farm	Location	Kind of soil
Usage of acreage	House description	Conveniences, roads
Extra features	Topography	Stock and equipment
Condition of buildings	Out buildings	Price, terms
	Reason for selling	

Key Descriptive Words and Phrases

Excellent fencing	No paint needed	Paved road
Well-located electrical outlets	Electrified fencing	Only ____ minutes from town
Good drainage	Modern plumbing and deep well	Indoor machinery storage
Well-lighted yard	Tree-shaded house	High productivity record
Convenient workshop	Excellent subdivision possibilities	
School bus stops at house	Good water system	

Business Property for Sale

Ad Copy Essentials

Type of Property	Suggested best uses	Price and terms
Facilities	Location	Type of construction
Store	Size (square feet, frontage)	Rail siding
Warehouse	Age, condition	Loading dock
Office	Heating systems	Labor supply
Showroom	Air conditioning	Transportation
Garage	Availability	Elevator
Name, address, phone	Parking available	

Key Descriptive Words and Phrases

Minimum maintenance required	No parking problems	Reinforced floors
	Close to highways	Eye-saving lighting
	Air conditioned	Secured leases
		Easy loading

Employee parking lot	Landscaped approach	Low tax area
Outgrown by present owner	Clear span ceiling	Large windows
	Bright display areas	Fireproof
	Clean	Pleasant, modern decor

Business Property for Rent

Ad Copy Essentials

Type of Property	Location	Facilities
Store	Type of Construction	Rail siding
Warehouse		Loading dock
Office	Size (square feet)	Transportation
Showroom	Frontage	Elevator
Garage	Zoning	Parking
Suggested best uses	Heating, air-conditioning	Will decorate
Lease information	Amount of rent	Name, address, phone
Number of rooms		

Key Descriptive Words and Phrases

Fireproof	Sprinkler system	Reinforced floors
Ample parking areas	Easy loading	Priced to rent now!
Good natural light	High ceilings	
Attractive exterior	Near public transportation	Clear span ceiling
Well lighted	Will remodel to suit tenant	Prestigious location
Private location	Private parking	Fast elevator service
Modern lobby	Ideal professional environment	Private entrance
Will partition to suit	High traffic frontage	Transportation at door
24-hour building service		

Business Opportunities

Ad Copy Essentials

Type of business	Equipment, type and condition	Price and terms
Location (traffic, if important)	Growth possibilities	Earnings, identify gross or net
		Parking facilities

Stock or inventory	Size	Name, address,
Lease, length and	Number of	phone
amount of rent	employees	
Years established	Reason for selling	

Key Descriptive Words and Phrases

Be your own boss	Fast developing	Owner able to
Loyal clientele	area	retire
Room for	Will pay for itself	Beautifully
expansion	Good lease, low	equipped
Money in the bank	rent	Books tell a profit
Solidly established	Efficient operation	story
Exclusive lines	Location spells	
Willing to work?	success	
Plenty of parking	Valuable franchise	

Income and Investment

Ad Copy Essentials

Type of building	Number and size	Age of property
Apartment	of rental units	Monthly income or
Office	Leases in effect	percent return
Duplex	Price range of	Vacancy for owner
Furnishings, if	rentals	occupancy
included	Heating	Air-conditioning
Heating	Name, address,	Price, down
Location	phone	payment, terms
	Construction	

Key Descriptive Words and Phrases

You can retire on	Big returns plus a	Firm investment
this income	place to live	All rented
Nets ____% plus	Steady tenants	Pride of ownership
$_____ per year	Attractively	Near schools and
income	redecorated	transportation
Guaranteed income	Your dollars work	Easy to maintain
Easy to manage	harder	income
Lifetime of security	Here is your home	Location tenants
Leased to large	and income	like
corporation	Finest rental area	Good income
	Investor's dream	Low upkeep costs

Low down payment	High return	Plenty of parking
High return plus security	First time offered	Public transportation nearby
	The best step toward security	

Houses for Rent

Ad Copy Essentials

Location	Number of bedrooms	Name, address, phone
Construction	Architectural style	Other rooms
Age	Decor	Lot size
Garage	Furnishings, if any	Rent
Option to buy	Special conditions	Appliances
References exchanged		Lease required
		Deposit

Key Descriptive Words and Phrases

In well-kept residential area	Large, usable basement	Spotless modern kitchen
Trouble-free heating system	Beautifully landscaped	Labor-saving floor plan
Good schools and shopping nearby	Airy, well lighted	Clean, automatic gas heat
Immaculately clean	Freshly papered and painted	Next best to your own home
Safe area for children	Walk to school, church and work	Good design, good looks and good price
Get the most for the rent	Paneled recreation room	

Apartments for Rent

Ad Copy Essentials

Unfurnished	Age, construction of building	Children, pets allowed
Location	Single, double or multiple unit	Utilities included
Number and kind of rooms (especially extra bedrooms)	Stove and refrigerator furnished?	Kind of heat
		Air-conditioning (if available)
		Parking facilities

Convenience to transportation and shopping
Closets and storage
Utilities included
Lease
Price, deposit
Name, address, phone

Furnished
Location
Building construction
Number of rooms
Furnishings, condition, clean
Kitchen appliances
Utitlities paid

Rent (week or month)
Lease required, deposit
Name, address, phone

Key Descriptive Words and Phrases

Unfurnished
Year-round climate control
Recently redecorated
More like a home than an apartment
Quiet, residential neighborhood
Prestige address
Quiet, friendly neighbors
Big windows, lovely view
Meticulously maintained
Floor plan spells convenience
Sparkling kitchen and bath

Large, bright rooms throughout
Massive closets and storage area
Makes housekeeping easy
School, park, transportation nearby
Spacious rooms for your furnishings
Furnished
Furnishing you would be proud to call your own
Expensively furnished
All electric kitchen

Spotlessly clean
Recently purchased furnishings
Good taste throughout
Warm, homelike, clean
Bright and airy
Ample closet and shelf space
Ideal for newlyweds
Top quality furnishings
Close in, sleep an extra 15 minutes
Harmonious decor and furnishings
Immaculate

CLASSIFIED ADS

A classified ad section is usually published carrying both straight classified (line ads) and classified display advertising (boxed, with graphics).

Straight classified advertising columns present more than 30 different types of real estate opportunities listed under three basic headings: real estate, houses for sale and rentals.

Classified display ads provide visual attention-getting devices such as large type, different type faces, borders, reverse cuts, logo types and frequently an illustration or photo.

Some metropolitan newspapers feature suburban editions, which provide economical prime coverage of select markets. Complete and separate local news and classified sections are also usually available. Editorial real estate sections are regularly scheduled within some of the suburban and city editions.

A separate Sunday section, featuring business and financial news and trends, is usually available for display advertising. Obviously, this is not low-budget advertising, but for those selling prestigious property with a price tag to match, it provides impact that no other media can match. The sports section as well as the recreational living section has also proven successful for real estate advertisers placing display ads.

Let's get it right! You're spending thousands of dollars annually. Make sure your ads obtain optimum results by using the methods suggested and include the vital information considered important to the prospective buyer. The more factors you incorporate into your ads, the more your chimes will ring.

ACTION COMMITMENTS

I have read the previous chapter and realize I must do the following:

TO DO	TARGET DATE OF COMPLETION	ACTION COMPLETED
1.		
2.		
3.		
4.		
5.		
6. Meet with sales manager.		

10 Selling the Property

Meeting your clients' needs by selling their property is an emotionally satisfying aspect of your business. It reveals your skills as a professional in such areas as marketing property through ad and sign calls, qualifying buyers' and sellers' practical and emotional needs, knowing available inventory and proper methods of showing property and, of course, handling objections and closing successfully. Where does the sale start? A successful sale starts with you! Keep in mind the following characteristics of success.

1. *Attitude.* You must think success, not "I can't do it." How you feel about people and yourself will determine your success. Dale Carnegie defined success as the ability to establish long-lasting personal and professional relationships with people. He further defined success as being made up of 15 percent talent and 85 percent attitude.

2. *Your strength.* By *strength*, we mean both physical and mental.

3. *Persistence.* Everyone says no at first. How you accept this and persist will affect your success.

4. *Enthusiasm.* It has to be genuine.

5. *Determination.* You can't give up!

There are six stages to a sale:

1. Initial contact
2. Qualifying the buyers
3. Showing the property
4. Obtaining the offer
5. Presenting the offer
6. Relaying acceptance

The first stage, the contact, has been covered in earlier chapters. The remaining stages will be covered in the next two chapters. We will include additional material to develop further your knowledge in the techniques of selling.

HOW TO CLOSE

Closing is a decision-making process, which, when mastered, enables you to help your clients reach a decision. It is important to learn the different types of closing techniques and where and when to apply them effectively.

The successful salesperson moves in and closes the sale from the beginning. He or she exudes confidence that customers will buy and asks questions about size, area, schools, where to put the furniture and so on.

In other words, the salesperson builds a picture of the benefits the home and his or her service will give the clients. Asking for the order then becomes the most natural thing in the world; and the final close is made easy.

What Is Closing?   As mentioned earlier, the term *closing* refers to decision-making. By continually closing and using the different closing techniques, you help customers make up their minds on a previous indecision. You are taking them through the decision-making process without their necessarily knowing it.

Why Is Closing Necessary?   The most important factor in closing is one you should remember: fear. Most people have difficulty making decisions, and buying a house is a tremendous decision to make. They fear it; they will procrastinate. A home is the largest single purchase a person will make, and the decision is a big one.

When Do You Close? Anywhere and everywhere! It's as simple as ABC, which really means, "always be closing." Throughout your contact with your customers, you should be trial closing and leading them to the final close in such a way that they are unaware of what you are doing.

Remember: you are leading customers through the decision-making process, and by using trial closes from the beginning, you are establishing agreement leading to the final decision.

Where Do You Close? Anywhere! The customer usually sets the stage. You'll close when prospecting, when showing the seller your competitive market analysis, while on the phone with ad and sign calls, when going from door to door, when talking to the service station attendant, while conversing at a social gathering, while driving buyers to the property and while at the property.

Basic Steps of a Close

Action Step 1 Understand the need for closing: People do not like to make decisions.

Action Step 2 Recognize the buying signs. A verbal sign might be when the customers make a statement about something they like. A visual sign is one manifested by a customer's body language. He or she might become quite involved in looking around; this could indicate an interest in this property as compared with other homes.

Action Step 3 Make the decision for your customers and start closing in that direction: "Would a 60-day possession be all right, or would 30 days be more convenient?"

Action Step 4 Close on it. Ask the customers a question the answer to which you already know. This starts them agreeing.

Psychology of the Close

Following are five important points that will help you close successfully.

1. Lead the clients so they are unaware that you are closing.
2. Avoid causing fear in your clients when they are thinking of buying.
3. Avoid any negative or fear-producing words or phrases. Following are suggested alternatives to money terms and other fear-producing words.
   - *Cost:* Use *investment.*
   - *Price:* Use *total investment.*
   - *Down payment:* Use *initial investment.*
   - *Contract:* Use *agreement.*
   - *Sign:* Use *approve.*
   - *Deal:* Use *opportunity.*
4. Work against building insecurity in your clients:
   - Select words and phrases with which your clients are familiar; avoid using trade jargon.
   - Ask questions that the clients can answer; this makes them feel secure and relaxed.
   - Don't ask unanswerable questions; this makes them feel insecure.
   - Don't make a statement of fact you can't back up. This will damage your credibility with the customer.
   - Try to get the customer to state the fact. Then he or she will believe it.
5. Whenever you ask a closing question, *close your mouth!* The first one to talk loses. There is no pressure you will ever exert that will remotely resemble that of silence. If you close your mouth, one of two things can happen:
   - your clients go along with you, or
   - they will give you a reason for not going along.

Closing Question Techniques

A closing question is one for which the answer confirms that the customer has bought. Again, after you ask a closing question, close your mouth.

Alternative of Choice   Give your customers positive choices about their assumed purchase:

> "Would 10 A.M. be better, or do you prefer 3:00 this afternoon?
>
> "Would you want to take title as joint tenants, or as community property?"
>
> "Do you prefer a 20 percent initial investment, or a 10 percent conventional program?"
>
> "Would a 60-day possession be all right, or would 30 days be more convenient?"

Active Questions   An active question is one that assumes the customers already own the home and forces a decision they will make when they do buy a home. It answers the question, "where?" For example,

> "Mrs. Buyer, where would you place the game table?"
> "Mr. Buyer, where would you put your workshop?"

Tie-Downs   A tie-down is a simple but effective tool to obtain an agreement or isolate an objection. Make a statement confirming something the customers have already expressed and tie it down with a phrase such as, "don't you agree?", "isn't it?", "won't it?" or "couldn't it?"

> "The kitchen window provides a lovely view, *doesn't it?"*
> "The living room is just what you want, *isn't it?"*

Assumptive Tie-Downs   This is an assumption you, not the customers have made, which you voice, then tie down immediately.

> "This is just what you were looking for, isn't it?"
> "A floor plan of this kind would be just perfect for your family, *don't you agree?"*

Handling Objections

While you have been trial closing by asking closing questions, your clients may come up with a few objections. Objections are indications of the customer's interest, elimination of the property or putting off decision making.

Objections can be an opportunity for you. By overcoming the objections, you can lead into the final close. Very often, hearing an objection clarifies the fact that the customers are getting ready to decide and want your help.

Following are some techniques to use to overcome objections. It is important to remember that you should not use these techniques in a "punch" type of approach. Don't use a strong, loud voice or you'll lose your clients. Keep it conversational.

Switch Off   If the objection seems minor, ignore it when you first hear it. If it is brought up again, go through the benefits of the home (items the customers already agree about). They will see the benefits outweigh the objection, and it will take the proper perspective.

Changing Base   This means changing the basis from which the objection originates. For example, one person might feel the property is too far away to drive to work. Both buyers might love the home, and you know it is perfect for them and fills their needs. At this point, you help the objector change his or her perspective by asking whether the house is everything he or she wants. If the answer is yes, then ask, "Is it worth driving the distance from work to a home like this?" The answer will probably be another yes, because the customer is emotionally attached to the home.

Formula for Minor Objections

- Hear the customers out. (Feed it back to them.)
- Question it. (Is this the only objection?)
- Answer it. (Appeal to emotions.)
- Confirm it. (Do you agree?)

Formula technique closing allows the clients to answer their own objections. Objections dealing with money, cost, price and monthly payments tell you that you have the opportunity to close because the customers have no emotional objections to the home itself and are putting off the decision.

CLOSING TECHNIQUES

At this point, it is necessary for you to ask yourself how many times to take no for an answer before you believe it. The greatest of closers average their close on the fifth closing attempt. There are as many ways to get a yes as there are closes. Most people are afraid of being rejected. But if you don't ask for an order, you'll never get one! Remember: Cows don't *give* milk, you have to *take* it.

How To Test for Closing

- Ask an alternate choice question.
- Ask an erroneous conclusion question. Misconstrue what they've said before. They'll correct it and come closer to saying yes.
- If a buyer asks a question like, "Does the barbecue grill come with the home?" answer, "Would you like that to be part of the agreement?"

Some people use another very good technique to eliminate the buyers' fear of the deposit early. Before showing them property, the salesperson gives the buyers the actual deposit receipt or purchase and sale agreement, and tells them, "This is the agreement we will use when we find your home. Take it home, look it over and I'll be happy to answer any questions you may have." The salesperson has accomplished several important things:

- The buyers have become familiar with a contract without calling it that.
- The salesperson has established trust with the buyers. They won't fear being surprised with an overwhelming legal document at the time they have the weight of making a decision.
- The salesperson has eliminated the natural fear people have of signing a contract they don't feel they've looked at properly.
- The salesperson has already overcome a *major* objection of signing an unfamiliar document.
- The salesperson has conveyed to the buyers that they are going to find a home.

Order Blank Close

Action Step 1   Start every sale using this method.

Action Step 2   Ask questions whose answers can be entered on the deposit receipt or purchase and sale agreement.

Action Step 3   Start at the bottom of the contract and work your way up, leaving price and terms for last.

Action Step 4   Suggested language:

> "How will you and your spouse be taking title?"
> "What is your correct mailing address?"
> "What is your present phone number?"
> "What is your correct full name?"
> "Would you prefer to assume the existing loan?"

Similar Situation Close

This also is known as the "feel, felt, found" formula. Suggested language:

> "I know how you *feel*."
> "I *felt* the same way, and you know what I *found?*"

The "I'll Think It Over" Close

This is also known as the out-on-a-limb close. It is one of the most common objections you will come across, and fear *is* usually the only reason for it.
Suggested language:

> "That's fine. Obviously you wouldn't take your time thinking this over unless you were really interested, would you?"
> "I'm sure you're not telling me this just to get rid of me, so may I assume that you will give it very careful consideration?"
> "To clarify my thinking. . .what part of this transaction do you want to think over? Is it. . ." (Begin with items you know they are favorable toward and continue until they stop you with an objection about one of the items you mention. Then go into the "final objection close."

If there is no objection, go back to the *order blank*.

FINAL OBJECTION CLOSE

This is also known as the "saw-off-the-limb-close." Here's the formula along with examples.

STEP 1 *Hear them out.*

> *Buyer:* "The house is okay, but it's just too far from the highway—six miles."

STEP 2 *Sell them their objection.*

> *Salesperson:* "As I understand it, you feel the distance from the highway just isn't good enough to save you the time reaching work you think you have to save if you purchased in this area."
>
> *Buyer:* "That's right."

STEP 3 *Confirm the objection.*

> *Salesperson:* "Now that's the only thing standing between us, isn't it? I mean, if it weren't for the distance thing, you'd go along with me today, is that right?"
>
> *Buyer:* "Yes, I suppose so."

STEP 4 *Question it.*

> *Salesperson:* "Just to clarify my thinking, why do you feel this is so impossible in terms of distance?"
>
> *Buyer:* "Well, it's an extra six miles each way every day."

STEP 5 *Answer it.*

> *Salesperson:* "Isn't it true that today we measure distance in terms of time, not miles? I mean, six miles is really seven or eight minutes. Multiply that by two, and that means for less than the time of a coffee break each day, you could enjoy living in the neighborhood of your choice. Isn't that true?"
>
> *Customer:* "You know, I never thought of it that way."

STEP 6   *Confirm the answer.*

> *Salesperson:* "Now that completely settles that, doesn't it?"
>
> Customer: "You're right."
>
> *How would you have answered the objection if the gasoline cost of the additional distance was too much?*

STEP 7   *Close it!*

> *Salesperson:* "By the way, what is your correct mailing address?"
>
> *Get back to the order blank close!*

The more you practice the various types of closes the more natural you will sound using them. Before you know it you will be closing when you aren't making a conscious effort to do so.

THE CLOSING CHECKLIST

1. Closing is a *decision-making* process.
2. Remember the ABCs of closing: *Always be closing.*
3. Fear is the customer's greatest obstacle to decision making.
4. Use positive words or phrases to counter the customer's fears: approve, transaction, investment.
5. The most important ACTION for you to take after you've asked a closing question is to *shut up!*
6. The closing techniques that receive most successful results are "tie-down" and "assumptive tie-down" statements:

   "The kitchen window provides a lovely view, *doesn't it?*"

   "Don't you agree?"

   "Won't it?"

   "This is a good example of a tie-down question, *isn't it?*"
7. By giving your customers a deposit receipt or a purchase and sale agreement at the start of your relationship, you eliminate their fear of signing an unfamiliar document. It's very helpful to use the deposit receipt or purchase and sale agreement in making a final sale.
8. When the decision is made, close on it immediately.

ACTION COMMITMENTS

I have read the previous chapter and realize I must do the following:

TO DO	TARGET DATE OF COMPLETION	ACTION COMPLETED
1.		
2.		
3.		
4.		
5.		
6. Meet with sales manager.		

QUALIFYING THE BUYER

It is essential to understand that the qualifying process is the only procedure to ensure obtaining the right property for your prospect, to determine if your prospect has a need to buy, the capacity to buy and a knowledge of the market.

Qualifying is a major function of your job; the better you understand how the process works, the better you will perform it.

Where Do You Qualify?

On the Telephone   Use the telephone only as much as needed to determine readiness to buy, needs as to size and so on. Your prime objective is to get an appointment.

On the Telephone   Use the telephone only as much as needed to determine readiness to buy, needs as to size and so on. Your prime objective is to get an appointment.

In the Office   Attempt to determine knowledge, need and ability to buy; begin to establish rapport.

In the Car   Get a feel for buyer's likes and dislikes; develop further rapport.

At the Property   Determine what the buyer *really* wants.

What Is the Customer's Reaction?

Your first contact with the buyers must be handled properly or they will react negatively to your questions. Your approach to combat this natural reaction should be as follows:

- Establish rapport; find a common ground with them.
- Show a sincere and friendly interest in them.
- Find their emotional needs and give them what they need emotionally.
- Discuss practical needs last.

It is most important to separate the buyers' practical *needs* from what they *want*. As you come closer to showing them property, provide them with what they need; number of bedrooms, nearness to schools, home size and so on. When you actually show them property, they will give you further clues as to what they want; style of architecture, amenities, pool, etc. When you find the right combination of what they need and want, at a price they can afford, then you will have met their needs.

Remember that the more rapport you develop with your customers, the more information you will receive. Probe gently for their motivation. Build their trust in you that you are sincerely interested in them.

Some Qualifying Questions

The following are questions to use in qualifying. Remember to integrate them into normal conversation so as not to sound like an interrogation. Not all questions need to be asked at one time;

you can ask them in the office, in the car, at the property you are showing:

- How large is your family? What are the ages of your children? Tell me about your family.
- How long have you been looking for a home? Where? With whom (other salesperson or broker)? Did you see any home that appealed to you? Where is it located? Tell me what you like best. What did you dislike about it?
- Is there any particular reason you didn't buy it? Would you like to own that home?
- If you had a choice of moving farther out to get the home you want, would you be willing to drive an extra 10 minutes to work or would you rather have a smaller, older home close to your place of employment?
- Have you set aside an additional three to four percent for closing costs?
- If I find an exceptional home that will require $2,000 to $4,000 more in down payment, should I show it to you?
- What monthly payment would you feel comfortable with?
- How high a monthly payment could you make for an exceptional home?
- Would you live in *this* home?
- Would you like to go through the home a second time?
- If you feel the price is too high, what would you pay for this home?
- Possible listing: Will you need to sell before you buy a new home?
- What did you and your family like about your last home? Was there anything you disliked in your last home?
- Describe your dream home to me.
- How soon do you need possession?
- In which area do you prefer to live?
- What are your requirements in a new home? What specific features will you require in your new home?
- Open-ended: Do you own your present home, or are you renting? Tell me about your present home.
- Which is more important to you: the condition of the home or the size and floor plan?

- Where does your spouse work?
- Do both of you work?
- Have you ever purchased a home before? Has anyone shown you how to purchase and finance a new home?
- How much of your savings have you set aside for your initial investment?
- Of the three homes we saw today, which did you like the best? Why?
- If I could arrange the financing so you could afford this home, would you buy it?
- Are you a veteran?
- When would you like to take possession?

By using the previously stated qualifying questions in a pleasant manner, you have established their needs, wants and ability to become involved in a particular property.

▼ ACTION RECALL

Qualifying the Buyer

Objective: Determine if the buyer has
- a need to buy.
- capacity to buy.
- knowledge of the market.

Steps:
- Determine family needs (bedrooms, etc).
- Determine needs for area (schools, etc).
- Pinpoint timing; when does the buyer wish to take possession?
- Inquire about wants versus needs.
- Determine financial capacity to make initial investment and monthly payment.
- Ask if buyer rents or owns.

ACTION COMMITMENTS

I have read the previous chapter and realize I must do the following:

TO DO	TARGET DATE OF COMPLETION	ACTION COMPLETED
1.		
2.		
3.		
4.		
5.		
6. Meet with sales manager.		

SHOWING PROPERTY

The objective of this section is to help you develop an understanding of the ACTION stage-setting steps you should take to help your buyers make favorable decisions about the home you show them.

Every successful merchant knows how important it is to display merchandise in ways that dramatize the features, benefits and values of what they have to offer, and thus set the stage for stimulating the interest of potential buyers. Successful real estate salespeople use similar techniques when selecting and showing homes to prospective buyers.

Motivations, Not Specifications

There is often a very substantial difference between what prospective buyers say they want and what they finally select.

To be successful, you must be able to detect the basic underlying desires that will determine the patterns of response and thus help you select the properties that are best suited to your buyers' real "hot buttons." As you continue probing throughout your relationship with the customer, search for the hidden clues that will be vital factors in consummating any transaction.

The counseling and qualifying sessions you conduct prior to the selection of any homes you plan to show are critical to the success of your personal sales routine.

By pursuing questions that uncover a prospect's attitude, knowledge and experience about real estate, you reduce the risk of spending a lot of time without achieving positive results. By asking the right questions, you produce the right answers.

Don't be in a rush to lose a sale. Some salespeople lose sales by becoming anxious to get to the properties before they've gotten to the buyers' motivations and reached an understanding as to their real interests and abilities. If it becomes obvious that your buyers do not know the ropes or are in need of additional education, it is usually better to invest the time to reinforce the essential elements of their understanding rather than to dash out, showing properties without adequately preparing them for the decisions they will be asked to make.

The effective real estate salesperson must achieve the following:

- Cultivate a high degree of empathy for the customers.
- Be extremely sensitive to their attitudes and reactions.
- Help anticipate and measure major motivations toward which you can tailor your efforts during the showing sessions.

The Elements of Showing Property

It is most important for you to understand the principles involved in showing property. They are as follows:

- Respect the buyer's viewing limit.
- Understand how decisions are made.
- Start from the buyer's position.

- Recognize that emotions are more important than facts.
- Employ the process of elimination.
- Every home is a compromise.
- Preview your properties.
- Plan your sequence.
- Show off the home.
- Don't defend the property.
- Handle objections.
- Show the home to its advantage.
- Get the buyer involved.

Respect the Buyer's Viewing Limit   How many homes should you select to show to any given client in one day? Real estate salespeople have vigorously discussed this question for years. Most who have been in the business for some time have concluded that it is unwise to show more than three to five homes in any single showing sequence and never that many if the job can be done with less. Why is this true?

The buyer finds it difficult to choose when faced with too many choices. It's like going into a restaurant and studying a menu with a hundred entrees. You'll really have a hard time deciding what to eat. When overwhelmed with too many things to think about or debate or discuss, the tendency is to postpone the decision—sometimes indefinitely.

When presented with too many listings, buyers lose their ability to remember them clearly. It's a condition called "house indigestion."

Alert real estate salespeople do everything in their power to avoid creating such situations. They realize their buyers have to be prepared for what they are going to see and they must aim for a limited number of properties that meet their motivations, abilities and needs.

Understand How Decisions Are Made   Buyers must think about and evaluate numerous details before making a commitment. To sell property, you must confirm many small decisions to pave the way for the major ones. An example of this is seen in the building of a bridge. Each little area of agreement represents another plank in the bridge; when all the planks have been securely nailed down, their structure is successfully completed. You have bridged the gap between buyer and seller.

One of your primary roles as a real estate salesperson is to bring buyers to an agreement. Each step of the way, you must consciously reinforce the positive factors that lead to the sale and thus dilute or eliminate negative ingredients that might destroy it.

Selling is an art based on the science of human psychology. The more you learn about human nature, and the way people react, the easier it will be for you to influence your buyers, sellers and associates in positive ways.

Start from the Buyer's Position   The foundation of any property sale is the customers' preconceived notions of what they are seeking. They have certain thoughts and experiences, motivations and abilities on which to build the agreement. Before you take the very first step or try to nail down the first plank, you must examine this foundation.

- What are they thinking at this point in time?
- How much experience have they had?
- What is the degree of urgency, ability, status, motivation?
- With what will they identify and why?

Salespeople often make the mistake of attempting to obtain decisions from their buyers before they have even established the criteria on which those decisions will be made. That's why the first step in selecting and showing homes and ultimately closing the sale is efficient counseling and qualifying. It is wise use of time and energy to invest more effort in these early sessions with your clients rather than to waste the energy and effort doing it the hard way as a result of not having the facts at the beginning. The more you really know and understand buyers, the easier it is to build a solid bridge to an agreement.

Recognize That Emotions Are More Important Than Facts   Another point that's worth stressing is the simple truth that emotions always play a greater role than facts in decision-making, although you must use both to build the bridge to an agreement. As salespeople, we must recognize that indecision is one of our greatest enemies. Everything we do is with the intent of helping customers reach favorable and positive decisions and avoid the frustrating dilemmas of confusion and uncertainty. How can we do this effectively?

We do it best when we remember that all customers buy on emotion and justify with facts. Never reverse that process. Putting facts before emotion is like putting the cart before the horse. When we see something for sale, it does not matter how much it costs, who made it or how well it is constructed *until we like it*.

Never try to sell anything until the customers show some evidence of interest and a degree of emotional involvement with it. When you try on a piece of clothing that you don't like, the salesperson can talk all day long and not change your feelings. In truth, that salesperson will quickly lose all opportunity to sell you that garment or anything else.

Remember the following when showing homes:

- Never debate room size, price or comparative values before you have ascertained the customer's attention and interest.
- Never defend a property to a buyer; doing so is a sure way to destroy a communicative relationship.
- Save your facts and your knowledge to help nail down the planks of agreement once you have received evidence of genuine emotional response.

Employ the Process of Elimination   Selecting a home is really a process of eliminating other possibilities. You first start with an entire community to choose from, then a neighborhood, then possibly three to five homes, then one or two and finally, as the attention and interest develop around one property, the others fade into insignificance.

Does the salesperson control this choice? YES! You help make the selection of the properties to be shown, you plan the sequence of showing and you help the buyers eliminate those that do not fit their needs, abilities and motivations.

At the beginning of your qualifying interview, you open many doors to learn all the things you must know if you are to serve your client properly. However, when you have the facts on the table, you begin closing the doors by shutting out those things that will not work. You eliminate the majority of your listings without the client ever seeing them. You do this mentally or by carefully reviewing the pictures and property description cards in your listing book.

The more accurate you are in selecting the best offerings that meet the needs and motivations you've been able to uncover, the easier it is to obtain a favorable decision on one property. You must first make some decisions before you ask your clients to do so:

- What are you going to show?
- Why are you going to show it?
- How many are you going to show?
- In what sequence will you show them?
- How can you best set the stage for the decision you want them to reach?

You should think through these important factors before dashing off to show some houses. Planning and preparation are among the major differences between the actions of a professional and those of an amateur in your business.

Every Home Is a Compromise   One of the other truths we have learned to appreciate is that there is no perfect home and that decisions are made ultimately by acceptance of reasonably good compromises. Buyers always envision more than they will finally buy, and they will give you specifications based on this vision. They ultimately make decisions to buy particular homes, however, because those homes satisfy basic emotional and financial needs outside of their extensive list of musts.

What will they compromise on and which motivations will play the key roles? Your mission is to uncover and interpret these elements before you are too far down the path to an exhausting tour of properties. Listen to what your clients tell you, and then listen for what they mean. Few of us are so skilled at communicating our thoughts to others that we really can say all we mean. Your responsibility is to act as a translator—to determine how their words and actions translate into what they want to buy.

Preview Your Properties   After you have decided on the few listings that might fit your buyers' needs, it's wisest to inspect them before showing them to your clients. Why? Consider the following good reasons:

The sellers might have changed their minds.   The only thing permanent in the real estate business is change, and that includes sellers who change their minds. You must know the exact status of a listing before exposing a potential buyer to it. Price, terms, possession dates and seller attitudes are critical to the negotiating stages. If you show a property to a prospect without knowing that possession has been changed or prices have been adjusted, you may present an offer that is totally unacceptable, or, worse yet, fail to get a decision to make an offer because you did not have the necessary ammunition.

You want the seller to be on your side.   If you have to bring the seller a less-than-acceptable offer, it pays to have a foundation of good will or rapport with which to work. Your expressed interest in the seller and the property can be of immeasurable value when you are in the final negotiating stages. By inspecting the home before you show it, just to refresh your memory, you can build a better relationship for this potential sale or the next one. Even if your showing does not result in a specific offer on the property, you will have made a better impression of your professional service and have created the potential sale for some other buyer you introduce later.

You can prepare the seller.   If this is one of your own listings, it is hoped that you have conditioned and educated the sellers in advance to the roles they should play in helping to show their home to its advantage. If it is not your listing, then you need to be sure they are prepared to do those things which will be important in the showing process.

After introductions, the seller should, if possible, leave the home to you for private inspection with your clients. Explain to the sellers that buyers are hesitant to express themselves when owners are too close, and you would not be able to have the freedom of the home to help the buyer overcome emotional obstacles.

Any disturbing influence should be eliminated; television sets should be turned off and children sent out to play. The house should be made to feel like a restful, relaxed environment in which the prospective buyer will feel at home.

Any negative condition should be corrected if it's going to be noticeable. Certainly, basic housekeeping rules apply, but obvious deficiencies can be overcome with careful planning.

Uncover the salable features. When you're looking at a home with particular buyers in mind, you can directly relate to what they will see, and the things that will be important to them. With those points in mind, you can ask questions of the seller that will uncover these areas. For example, if your prospects have children, it would be helpful to know whether or not the neighbors have children, their ages, etc. If this is a plus, you would like to uncover it and use it to help reinforce the prospect's interest in the property when you bring him to that location.

A serious word of caution should be mentioned at this time. If the listing is not yours, that is, you do not represent the seller, you must exercise a great deal of caution when contacting the seller. Consult the policy of your office and the local Board of REALTORS®.

It's very difficult to be totally knowledgeable about all your properties, and refreshing your own information just prior to showing gives you the edge over the salesperson who carelessly exposes merchandise without knowing all the vital details.

Plan Your Sequence   If you have selected three properties to show, which one should be shown first, and why? Experienced salespeople approach this problem from two viewpoints: One group likes to begin with the least probable choice, and conclude with the best one; the other group likes to start with the best and show the others, only if necessary, returning to the first home a second time if the other two properties are not right.

Both methods work well. It depends on the type of buyers and your own selling techniques. A salesperson should plan the showing sequence based on a knowledge of the buyers' attitudes, experience and motivations.

For example, if the buyers have already seen a number of homes with other agents and you are fairly certain you have one listing that will best suit their requirements, it would be unwise to show other properties at all. On the other hand, if some conditioning, educating or comparison is required to set the stage for the right listing, it would be best to start with the other properties. That will help the buyers appreciate by direct identification the one you feel they should buy.

Sometimes you have to show a home or two that are less attractive to give your buyers the the full impact of the one you believe they should own or to educate them to the realities of the market. Whatever sequence you decide to use, the showing plan should be structured to help you obtain a positive decision and eliminate confusion.

Plan the routes to the properties.   The approach to a home is like the musical introduction to a show. It prepares the audience for what is to come and emotionally stimulates interest in the events that follow.

It is true that showmanship is part of life, and certainly is an important function in the selling process. When a jeweler is trying to sell you an expensive ring, he does not drop it into your hand and say, "Here it is." The successful merchant knows the value of putting the jeweled setting on a velvet pad and placing it under a bright light where each delicate facet can reflect its brilliance to the observer. Most of us appreciate the refinements of living that add zest and interest to our otherwise uneventful routines.

Allow enough time. The search for a home should be a relaxed and pleasant experience. After all, the buyers will invest many years and enjoy memories accumulated from the pleasures of living there. As you plan showing appointments, always allow enough time between listings for the buyers to really absorb what they are seeing. If the showing process is hurried or pressured in any way, the buyer may not have time to become mentally involved. Buyers must move in mentally before they buy the property; that requires the emotional stimulation that will take them from a passive state to an active one.

Employ the element of discovery. The steps to a sale are always up, never down. The elevator to success is out of order; you must do it one step at a time. You lead your clients up each stair until the ACTION point has been reached. Whenever you reverse this process, you fail. The element of discovery is vital to the emotional impact the property produces on the prospect's mind and heart.

Start slowly and build interest as the visual experience of the property and its benefits begin to work on the emotions of the buyer. If you tell your client too much beforehand, you remove some of the closing tools you could use and you deny him or her the privilege of discovery.

Prepare the buyer. Before you start out on any showing appointment, it is wise to take a few moments to prepare your buyer.

First of all, put the buyers at ease. Let them know you're not going to try to sell them anything, but rather, you want to offer a full opportunity to view the properties you have selected for their inspection. By removing any psychological pressure under which the buyers might be placed, you help them get in the mood to see, feel and respond to the homes you will show.

Second, it is unwise to tell the buyers how many homes you have chosen that day. Leave this to the imagination. If you say that you're going to show five homes, and you're on number three, and that's the one they should buy, the buyers are still going to want to see numbers four and five. Keep this element under your own control.

Next, it helps to suggest that buyers take notes to remember elements of the properties. Some salespeople keep pencils and notebooks or writing tablets in their cars for this purpose. To help them remember what they have seen, suggest they jot down some key points in the car before they move on to the next property.

On the way to the property.   There are four basic objectives to be accomplished as you proceed to the property.

- Continue qualifying buyers for all areas of information you have not yet secured.
- Reinforce real estate values in the area that you plan to show.
- Sell the buyers on the neighborhoods and the people in the immediate area of the properties you plan to inspect.
- Prepare the buyers for any obvious negatives they may see, and get them mentally ready for the discovery of the home you plan to show.

The last point needs further emphasis. Many salespeople take away their own ammunition by telling the buyers all about the home they are going to see before they get there. As previously emphasized, you must make the element of discovery work for you. Do not tell the buyers how great it's going to be; let them discover it. If there is a negative, however, something that the buyers will obviously realize upon arrival, it's best to prepare them for it. Imagination works in reverse. If you tell them something is not quite as satisfactory as they might like, they will usually picture it as being worse than it really is. Conversely, if you gloss over the negatives, the buyers will likely be disappointed, and you will have taken away the potential for their involvement in the property's benefits.

Sell the neighborhood and community before the property.
People do not buy houses, they buy neighborhoods, communities, people; in other words, a way of life. A home cannot be isolated from its total environment.

If you want to sell a specific home, you must first sell the neighbors, schools, parks and community resources. The neighboring homes and the people who live there are part of the new environment the buyers are considering. Tell them about the advantages of this particular community or neighborhood.

On the way to the listing you have selected, pick out the features that will emphasize the benefits of living in this section of town:

- Where are the schools their children will attend?
- Are they good schools, with the best teachers and educational programs?
- Are there neighborhood parks where their children can play, or membership clubs in which the entire family can participate?

As you approach the property, you should also have stressed the created values that others are making to reinforce their interest in this specific community. If new shopping centers and buildings have been erected, discuss them and point out how these kinds of development contribute to the value of the homes they are reviewing.

Show off the Home   Unless the surrounding homes detract from the one you are going to show, always plan to arrive and park in a way that will let the buyers see the adjacent properties and yards at their best. Many times this objective is accomplished by parking across the street at an angle somewhat away from your listing.

As you step from the car, the buyers should be able to see the home as it's framed by the neighboring properties and accented by trees, lawns, shrubs and flowers. The buyers can then absorb the full impact of the setting as they approach the home. If there are exterior features that should be emphasized, now is the time to point them out.

As you reach the front door, set the stage for the showing by putting the buyers at ease. If the home is occupied, always protect owners and sellers alike from any potential embarrassment or discomfort that can result from the unexpected. If the owner is home, introduce your clients and let them precede you into the home. If the owner is not home, always enter first and be sure everything is all right before you continue the inspection.

Take your time. The inspection of a home should be a relaxed event for your clients. If it is conducted at a rapid pace, they will have neither the time to absorb the features nor the ability to focus attention on the items they are interested in.

Your job is to set the pace and maintain a psychological climate that will be favorable to your objectives. This is not the time for a bus tour. Let your buyers see, feel and identify with the home.

Silence is golden. If there is one time more than any other when you should do little or no talking, it is during the first inspection of a home. Too many salespeople feel the necessity to talk about the features of the homes they are showing before the buyers have been given the opportunity to react to the environment. While talking away, you interfere with the buyers' concentration and often prevent them from selling themselfves on the property through the subtle impact of their emotions and responses.

If you say anything, it should be only to point out some feature they might otherwise miss, and even this should be kept to a minimum until they have been through the home completely.

As we stressed earlier, we always buy on emotion and then justify with facts. Don't use your facts at a time when they have no relevance. If you use them prematurely, you can destroy the emotional environment in which the mental processes are allowed to work for you.

Don't Defend the Property   Don't argue with buyers about the value of a property; you may win the argument, but lose a friend and a sale.

If a buyer makes adverse comments about some aspect of the property, don't try to prove him or her wrong or emphasize the benefits of the property. By doing so, you risk shutting off the buyer's mental receivers and destroying your opportunity of communicating. Before you respond, keep the following points clearly in mind.

- Any observation that is made before the entire property has been seen is not really important. Every home is a compromise, and the objections on one point might well be offset by the benefits of other features.

- To debate or defend an objection is to risk reinforcing it in the buyer's mind. What might have been only a minor and relatively insignificant comment can become a major stumbling block because of the premature emphasis you've allowed it to gain.

- Buyers often solve their own objections if given the opportunity to do so. What they need is merely the time to adjust to the compromises and think things through. If you act as a sounding board rather than as a person who has to dominate the scene, you will accomplish much more.

If you are by chance in the wrong home and your buyers do not have a genuine interest in it, you may build a barrier by defending or justifying the property. Never take the chance of losing good buyers just because you feel the necessity to talk.

Handle Objections An objection can be any one of the following:

- A request for more information
- A mere comment or observation
- An attempt to slow down an imminent decision
- A genuine problem

For more information on this subject, refer to "How To Close," earlier in this chapter.

Because it is seldom possible to know the real motive behind the objection when it is first made, it is always wisest to explore the situation before jumping to conclusions. Much depends on how and when the objection is made.

For example, if the buyers are just starting through a home with you and they make an observation that a particular bedroom is too small, the comment should not be important until the entire property has been inspected. Possibly other elements of the home will overshadow this objection. As they stand in the living room and view the setting sun from a picture window, the bedroom and its size may fade into insignificance.

Always remember that the process of buying or selling real estate represents making many decisions and minor compromises before ultimate decisions are reached. By concentrating on the objection prematurely, you can actually help make it a real objection when it could have been only a minor one.

Unless the objection comes up at a time when you are closing the sale, it is safest to bypass the comment until the entire story has been presented. Many sales experts insist that some objections are not critical factors in a sale until they have appeared twice or come up in closing.

If objections need to be addressed then, before answering, it's always wise to question the objections. The salesperson who answers an objection impulsively before questioning it creates a defensive climate and usually overshoots the mark.

Before telling what you know, find out what the other person knows. Give the buyers a chance to express themselves in a climate of interest which you maintain by your attitude and actions.

There are many benefits to questioning an objection before you answer it. First, the true nature of the objection may not be evident. Second, when given a chance, buyers frequently address their own objections.

There are several steps involved in handling adverse comments or objections:

1. Ignore it if the buyers have not seen all the property, or unless it comes up twice.
2. Evaluate it in terms of other interests as to whether it is a genuine objection.
3. If it needs to be solved, never answer until you question the buyer about it.
4. After questioning it, confirm the objection by restating it again and give the buyers a second chance to see it in proper perspective and possibly develop solutions.
5. Then, if necessary and important, answer it, but always in a question form such as, "Had you considered this possibility?", "How would this work?" or "Suppose we did this. . ."

Showing the Home to Its Advantage   Is there a special way a home should be shown? Most real estate experts indicate there is no single way a salesperson should show a home. There is value, however, in trying to route buyers so you save the best for last.

Certain rooms in any home will show better than others, and it is practical to use these as closing tools. Selling works best when it's a natural staircase relationship of desire that leads to ACTION. Any showing technique that accents this natural selling process will usually be more effective in achieving the ultimate objective.

Some salespeople prefer to start with the bedrooms and end the tour in the living area where the benefits are usually the greatest. You cannot always control the buyers, however. Your own judgment must relate to their actions and attitudes.

If the home is occupied and the owner is absent during the showing, always precede the buyers into the sleeping wing and open doors for them to be sure to avoid any unpleasant scenes.

When you are taking clients into small rooms, avoid accenting the size by your own presence. If you stand in the middle of a small bedroom, it will appear to be even smaller. Your own visual height will detract from the real dimensions. It is best either to avoid entering the room at all or to stand against the wall so you blend into the environment as much as possible. Small bathrooms opening off a hallway always appear much larger if the light is turned on.

Never stand in front of a window. This breaks the view and extends the eye and the light to the outside.

During the showing process, your chief role is to watch, listen and interpret the buyers' reactions and observe carefully. Observe the buyers' expressions as they discover each area of the home. If they make comments, try to evaluate them and avoid the tendency to answer and relate the comments to the background of information you have already gathered.

Pay particular attention to any visual or oral signs of interest. If they comment that something is nice, immediately agree with them, but don't give a lecture on the subject. Let them absorb the scene and respond to what they see in their own way.

Remember all their positive reactions and be prepared to feed them back in the closing summary, if this is the right house. Your own alertness can be a major advantage in your closing efforts.

It is difficult, if not impossible, to listen and talk at the same time. Your safest bet is to keep your mouth shut, your ears open and your brain in gear. Someone once made the observation that, God made each of us with two ears and one mouth, which is a sign that we were intended to do twice as much listening as talking. That's a very good rule for a real estate salesperson to follow.

Get the Buyer Involved   Selling is based on the art of involvement. Buyers have to identify with it, imagine owning it and become sufficiently involved with the emotional benefits that they are willing to take the final ACTION.

What is involvement?   Involvement is the emotional identification with the product, the benefits of ownership and the protection of your own feelings related to the environment. When buyers begin to visualize living in a home, to see their children playing in the backyard and feel the sensations of the environment, they begin to get involved. That's how all selling is done, regardless of the product.

Homes are sold when people mentally move into them. When buyers begin to picture their furniture in a room and drapes on the windows, when they see themselves relaxing in a wood-paneled den, they are moving in. The easiest way to sell any home is to let the buyers get involved with it and then to reinforce their emotions with whatever facts will fit their own personalities.

The second look. One of the most effective closing tools in home selling is the simple but powerful question, "Would you like to go through the home again?" By allowing the buyers the privilege of seeing the home once more before they leave, you can help them complete the mental involvement which has already begun.

Many times, it is wise to let the buyers make this second inspection alone, while you talk to the owner or otherwise occupy yourself. Their private conversations may well allow each to confirm what the other has suspected, but did not want to express in your presence: that they liked the house. Wives can often do the job of selling their husbands much better than you can ever do.

Successful salespeople are sensitive to the responses and emotional reactions of buyers. They have a sense of timing, and know how to use it to advantage. Experience will teach you these refinements, provided you are willing to tune up your antenna and your mental equipment.

The wrong house. What do you do if you quickly sense you are in the wrong house? This is not the home these buyers want, and it is obvious in their attitudes and actions. First of all, cut the inspection short. Don't waste time and emotional energy in the wrong environment. When you return to your car, take a few moments to acknowledge your recognition of their reactions and then question what features they did not like. You may uncover something that you missed previously. You need to know for sure so as not to make that same mistake again.

If you missed something in your qualifying and counseling, now is the best time to get it out on the table. As in the game of baseball, too many strikes and "you're out!"

Summary Let's review the elements of showing property:

- Respect the buyer's viewing limit.
- Understand how decisions are made.
- Start from the buyer's position.
- Recognize that emotions are more important than facts.
- Employ the process of elimination.
- Recognize that every home is a compromise.
- Preview your properties.
- Plan the sequence.
- Show off the home.
- Don't defend the property.
- Handle the objections.
- Show the home to its advantage.
- Get the buyer involved.

▼ **ACTION RECALL**

Showing Property

Objective: Based on financial needs, actual needs and emotional wants, to select homes, one of which you feel the buyer will purchase.

Steps:
- Sell the home on the way: its advantages, and the average price range, ages, features and amenities of surrounding homes.
- Park across the street, if home has good curb appeal.
- Allow buyers to "discover" the home. Let them go at their own pace, but stay near to guide and answer questions.
- Point out what you want them to notice, if they missed it.
- Ask active closing questions: tie-downs, alternatives of choice.
- Answer questions with questions. Don't misrepresent the property.
- Eliminate all but one house.

Suggested Language: "Feel free to go through the house. I'll answer any questions you may have." (Lead them or follow close behind.)

Minor Objections: "Yes, I noticed that, but. . . (and switch off).

Closing Questions: "Where in this comfortable den would you put your favorite chair?"

"Would this wall or the west wall be best for your art display?"

Answer Questions with Questions: "You really do like the open feeling in this kitchen, don't you?"

"Would you like the fireplace equipment to stay? We can make that part of the agreement."

Eliminate Other Homes: "Of the three homes we've seen today, which did you like best?"

Go Back to the Office (if appropriate timing): "Let's go back to the office where I can give you the information you requested."

- Give the information requested.
- Start filling in order blank (deposit receipt or purchase and sale agreement).
- Close for agreement.

ACTION COMMITMENTS

I have read the previous section and realize I must do the following:

TO DO	TARGET DATE OF COMPLETION	ACTION COMPLETED
1.		
2.		
3.		
4.		
5.		
6. Meet with sales manager.		

11 Finalizing the Sale

All the showing, all the positive and negative reactions are worthless unless they culminate in an offer to purchase. The objective to keep in mind is that the buyers have to find a home of their choice. For sellers to dispose of their home through you, their agent, the buyer must offer to purchase the seller's home.

Previous chapters covered the groundwork leading up to making the offer. If you haven't read the material, now is the time to do so. See Chapter 10 to get a better understanding of the information to be presented in this section.

We will cover the following aspects of the offer in this section:

- Securing the offer
- Presenting the offer
- Representing both sides

SECURING THE OFFER

Buyers rarely volunteer to make offers, so it behooves the salesperson to suggest that the offer be made, but only when you, the adviser and counselor, sincerely believe that the home is the one the buyer should purchase. After having obtained and studied the buyer's qualifications, wants, needs and reactions, and you feel all or most of the factors are reasonably satisfied, you should proceed to obtain the offer.

Here's where your loyalty to purpose rewards you and the buyer: If you have been loyal, honest and conscientious to your buyers during the initial interviews and the showing of homes, and you have developed a rapport and invaluable confidence and recognition of your competent attitude, then when you come to the point of suggesting that they make an offer, the buyers will probably agree. This is because it's merely a continuation of the favorable reaction and attitude you and they developed, as you worked together to solve the problem.

Respect of you is essential. . . sincerity by you is paramount.

Consider the Buyer's Point of View

If the buyers don't agree with your suggestion, do not push. Consider their point of view, and find out how your viewpoints differ. Ask, listen and probe.

If you think the offer appropriate, suggest going back to the home again. You and your buyers are a *team* working together. Never lose that rapport because of a momentary difference of opinion.

Don't argue. Remember, they are the ones to live in the home, not you. They are working on facts plus emotion; you're working on facts alone. It is your duty, however, to be sure their facts are accurate. If they object strongly, then respect their feelings and continue with your search. Remember, if the people had no problems, we would have no business.

Handling Objections

Objections reflect interest, whether slight or great. A conscientious and successful salesperson attempts to sort the rational objections from the irrational ones, and places each in its rightful category, all with the idea of guiding the buyers to an accurate evaluation of their objections and opinions.

Questions should generally be answered with a question, for this helps the buyers answer their own questions and analyze their own doubts. All you are doing is guiding them in making their own decisions as you steer them with accurate facts.

Ask questions. This is another good method of handling objections. Frequently, this is referred to as "adding tie-downs." You present a query of a certain point or fact and the buyer is given an opportunity of agreeing or not agreeing to something you feel is a situation, a condition or a fact. An example would be, "You really do need four bedrooms, don't you?"

Handling objections has been covered in depth in Chapter 10. For more information, review this chapter.

Closing with Explanation of Financing

Financing is the true key to whether or not obtaining a desired home can become a reality. At the point when the offer is made, the subject of financing must receive full attention and be given crystal-clear on paper as well as in conversation. In your qualifying interview, or in subsequent early discussions, you learned thoroughly the buyers' financial qualifications and capabilities, as well as their knowledge of and attitudes toward loans.

You must be certain from the very first meeting that the buyers understand the language of basic financing terms so that psychologically they aren't biased against normal financing techniques.

You have also learned previously all existing financial data on the home being considered for purchase. You know precisely what the existing loan is on the home and what type of financing is available. You know whether a second mortgage would be available through the seller. These are essential facts you should be aware of before offer-writing time.

It is helpful and reassuring for buyers to have paper and pencil (which you provide), so they can follow your figures and suggestions as you explain them. It really allows them to see how the home looks "on paper."

While working the financing with them visually, try to begin with the listed price, for it establishes loan value. If the down payment and monthly payments are found to be too high, then the figures can be reworked at a lower sale price.

Writing the Offer

This is negotiation time. Writing the offer is a vital step in the art of bringing buyer and seller together. It is matching what one is willing to receive or give up, to compare advantages of owning a certain home against what one is willing to pay to assume the advantages of owning that home.

When disclosing facts, be sure they are accurate. The competitive market analysis serves this purpose, both when listing and at the time of the offer.

In setting down on paper the suggested and practical formula for financing the home, do it simply. The buyer right now, and the seller later, do not want to be subjected to confusing and overwhelming arrangements. Keep it simple. Do not cause mental indigestion by giving buyers and sellers too many unfamiliar facts too quickly.

Present the variables as follows:

- Put down the total price.
- Subtract the cash down payment.
- Point out the balance to be financed.
- Break down the financing into the components as necessary.

During the procedure, you have invited the buyers to follow you on a scratch pad. Let them follow your review of the amortization book for the loan figures. As you progress, ask them periodically if they agree with your figures.

After you have thoroughly advanced to the completion of financing, develop the offer on the deposit receipt or purchase and sale agreement; ask for their approval, not for them to "sign here."

Once you have developed the offer, whether it is for full price or at a lower price, take it to the seller as soon as possible, but only after you have determined the alternate conditions your buyer will accept in the event the seller doesn't agree to the offer as it appears.

Preparation for Presenting the Offer

Action Step 1   Prepare the buyers to fail. Indicate to the buyer that there may be other offers on the home or that conditions in the offer may not be acceptable to the seller. However, you most certainly do not want to lead them to believe you will be shopping for a counteroffer.

Action Step 2 Determine where your buyers will be and how you can contact them in the event that you have to reach them. You may get a reaction from the sellers, and time will be of the essence to finalize the transaction.

Action Step 3 Call the listing agent or broker to set an appointment for presenting the offer. If the listing agent requests to see the offer prior to submitting it to the sellers, suggest you meet the agent in front of the property and review it there, or pick the agent up, and allow him or her to review it on the way to the property.

Why? If the agent reviews it at his or her office, he or she might call and present it over the phone. Maintain control of your offer.

Action Step 4 Memorize your offer. Review the listing information and comparables. Look for any needs the sellers had indicated that your offer can fill that will sound good to the seller. Memorize all conditions. You will probably not have the agreement before you to refer to at all times.

PRESENTING THE OFFER

When you present an offer to the sellers, you owe them the same candor and full disclosure you gave the buyer. Sincerity and honest opinion have always propelled people further down the road to success and to the maximum satisfaction of all parties concerned.

This portion is divided into two parts, "When You Are Working with the Buyer," and "When You Represent the Seller."

When You Are Working with the Buyer

Before we move into the techniques of the presentation itself, it is important to note that your mental and physical attitude going into the presentation will determine to a large degree its outcome. How you perceive what you are about to do is vitally important.

If you convey in your manner and physical gestures the attitude of an apology for the offer you are presenting, you are inviting a rejection of the offer maybe even before you have made the presentation. Your entire bearing must convey confidence and a positive attitude toward the news you are bringing to the sellers.

You are setting the stage, and it must appear positive in order to receive a positive reaction from the seller.

Let's look at the techniques of making the presentation:

- Arrive at the property; introduce yourself to the sellers and the agent, if you have not previously met.
- Select the proper room. If you sit in the living room, people are split up; they sit in scattered areas, and there is no convenient table to write on. Try to guide them to the kitchen or dining room table. Here, everyone is close together; it is easy to pass papers around; the deposit check can be displayed and kept visible; and it's easy to sign documents, calculate figures and pass the pen.
- What are some bad opening statements?

    "I realize this is not a very good offer, but my buyer said, "Try!""

    Or

    "I realize it's not a very good offer, but we are hoping for a good counteroffer." (Any mention of counteroffer at all is very poor.)

    Or

    "Why would anyone want to leave such a lovely home?"

- What are some good opening statements?"

    "I'm happy to present you with the highest price ever obtained for this floor plan." (Or on this street, or in the area, etc.)

    Or

    "I think you will be pleased with the deal." (Notice the word "deal" is used instead of "offer" to avoid giving the impression that an offer is an invitation to a counteroffer.)

    Or

    "I have a well-qualified buyer and a clear, straight forward offer to purchase."

Objection to Price   If you have gone through all the minor objections and filtered the sellers down to their final objection and that objection is price with no way to counter that objection further, you have two choices:

1. Accept the rejection of the offer, knowing for certain that your buyers will not and cannot accept any other terms.
2. Go for an acceptable counteroffer.

"Let's remember, we do have a well-qualified buyer who is willing and able to purchase."

"Let's see if we can keep this together."

"Let's see if we can get essentially what you want and what they want." "Let's see if we can keep this alive."

Go back to the positive points you determined earlier and restate them and gain their agreement. Get back down to the final objection, "price," and bring out your comparables for the area. This is where your knowledge of the area will help you negotiate a realistic and fair counteroffer.

When You Represent the Seller

Most of the education of the sellers and their role before and during the presentation of an offer should be gone over at the time of taking the listing and reviewed again, just prior to the presentation.

Instruct your sellers on the following:

Tell them not to discuss any offer, or the possibility of an offer, with any other broker. Any questions should de directed to you, the listing agent.

Inform the sellers that other agents can get valuable information with seemingly innocent conversation: "Where are you moving?" "When are you moving?" "Have you purchased another home?" "Why are you leaving such a lovely home?" Reinforce to them that any contact with the sellers should be directed to the listing agent.

If the selling agent contacts the sellers directly to present an offer, the sellers should redirect the agent to the listing agent. That is what they are paying you for.

Tell them how you will react at the time an offer is being presented. If you feel it is a good offer, you will tell them outright.

Let them know that if you feel there are items you want to discuss privately with them, you'll sit quietly. This will be a signal for the sellers to ask the agent presenting the offer if they may have time to discuss the offer in private. The agent will probably object, but you can step in and ask if he or she can wait in his or her car (not in another room). They can say, "Give us about ten minutes." You will then make your comments and suggestions to the sellers and draw a counteroffer while the agent is out of the home.

CHECKLIST FOR PRESENTATION OF OFFERS

Check "yes" or "no" for each answer.

Yes	No	
❏	❏	1. Ensure additional deposit in escrow.
❏	❏	2. Determine loan information.
❏	❏	Whether anticipated loan is realistic
❏	❏	Whether the loan will stay with lender of record
❏	❏	What the prevailing rate of interest is
❏	❏	Days required to obtain the loan
❏	❏	3. Purchase money first trust deed (if applicable).
❏	❏	Insurance coverage
❏	❏	Financial statement
❏	❏	Tax service
❏	❏	Acceleration clause
❏	❏	All due and payable in years
❏	❏	Rate of interest
❏	❏	Payable at $___ monthly

Yes	No	
☐	☐	4. Purchase money second trust deed (if applicable)
☐	☐	Tax service
☐	☐	Notice of default
☐	☐	Acceleration clause
☐	☐	All due and payable in _____ years
☐	☐	Rate of interest
☐	☐	Payable $____ monthly
☐	☐	5. Finalize escrow requirements
☐	☐	Company
☐	☐	Date of closing
☐	☐	Date of occupancy
☐	☐	6. Ascertain personal property included or excluded.
☐	☐	7. Ascertain time limit for removal of all contingencies.
☐	☐	Loan
☐	☐	Inspections, etc.
☐	☐	8. Multiple counteroffers.

▼ **ACTION RECALL**   **Presenting Offer to Sellers**

Objective: To consummate the sale.
Steps:

- Be prepared, update CMA; know time on market, offers, etc.

- Have someone make appointment with seller, if you're the listing agent.

At Appointment:

- Establish rapport, report good news, be positive, emphasize good points of buyer.

- Present parts of offer one at a time: possession, personal property, terms, price.

- Present least objectionable items first; most objectionable items last. Get the easy "Yes" first.

- Present the offer and close your mouth. The next step is the sellers'.

- Show total proceeds of sale.

- If there is strong objection, try to overcome by comparison.

- If sellers refuse, get counter in writing.

Suggested Language:

Offer: "I have some good news . . . we have a qualified buyer interested in your home. He has agreed to your possession date."

On Counter, if Necessary:

"What would you consider an acceptable offer?"

Relaying Counter Back to Buyers:

"I have some good news. Mr. and Mrs. Seller accepted. . . (Mention parts accepted). "They have also agreed to come down $___ on their price. Right now, you are the only ones who know you can purchase the home of your choice at this reduced price."

Then Close for Acceptance.

REPRESENTING BOTH SIDES

This situation, in which the same person represents both the seller and the buyer, is rather self-explanatory at first glance; it's important, however, to point out several things that may not be immediately apparent.

Say, for example, that the buyer is interested in making an offer on one of your listings and you are in the process of discussing the writing up of the offer. Suppose the listed price is, in your opinion, too high. Buyers come to you because you are a REALTOR® or a REALTOR-ASSOCIATE® who subscribes to a Code of Ethics that ensures an impeccable relationship. Do you owe the buyers an ethical obligation to tell them that you feel the price is above fair market value? The answer is yes.

At the same time, if you are the lister of the home, you are an agent of the sellers, the principals. You therefore have prime allegiance to the sellers to get the listed price for them. Are you being ethical to the sellers when you conscientiously tell the buyers the listed price is too high? The answer is yes, provided that when the home was listed, you gave the sellers this same opinion: that their listed price was above fair market value.

If you used the competitive market analysis (CMA), chances are the sellers respected your opinion and listed at fair market value (FMV). But suppose they didn't. Suppose they didn't agree with FMV figure and insisted on listing the home at their price. To them, it would take that much more than FMV to cause them to give up the privilege of owning and enjoying the home in the future. That is the sellers' privilege, for it is their home. All you have done is be fair to all parties.

If, however, other comparable homes offer competition and enable the buyers to purchase a similar home at a lower price, the CMA will explain to the seller why the buyers were not willing to pay as much as the sellers expected them to offer at the listed price.

When you told the buyers that the listed price was above FMV, you should also have explained that the listed price is what the sellers formally declared was required to deprive them of ownership; that it was subjective, not an objective price. The sellers have that privilege.

By being frank, you have gained the buyers' respect. If they still wish to offer the listed price, then they have recognized, as have the sellers, that the asthetics and desire reflect a price higher than the FMV. The buyers have become subjective and that is their prerogative, not yours, once they have the facts on FMV which you were obligated to give them.

The Deposit Receipt

Keep the deposit receipt in your hands while you are telling the sellers about the buyers and the elements of the offer.

Once you let go of the deposit receipt, you will have lost their attention, and they won't hear a word you're saying.

While you are holding it, you have their complete attention and can tell them about the buyers. Humanize them; make the sellers want them to have their home; have the neighbors happy they sold it to a good family.

After you have sold them on your buyers, hand them the deal and close your mouth. All they will be able to see is dollar signs. Wait for them to speak, no matter how long it takes.

Many an acceptable deal has been lost because the salesperson talked too much.

Possible Objections

Don't act too anxious to get a counteroffer if a minor objection is voiced. Use the same techniques you have learned in countering other objections; after all, the sellers are going through the decision-making process. Help lead them through the steps to agreement.

Attempt to draw out the positive responses from the sellers and their agent:

> "Is the escrow period satisfactory? Does it fit with your timing?"
>
> "As you can see, the buyers have agreed to stay with your lender, saving you. . ."

Lead them down the path of elimination of objections, questioning them, answering them. You will then come down to one of two conclusions: They accept the deal, or they reject the price offered.

If the buyers say "no, we won't even pay the FMV," you, nevertheless, should suggest a reasonable offer of whatever price they will pay. You have served them and you have also served the sellers, because you have created a potential negotiation, rather than no offer at all.

When they receive the offer, the sellers should be told exactly what you told the buyers. Review the CMA with them. If they refuse the offer, they have repurchased the home themselves, so to speak. That is their prerogative, for it is their home. At this point, you should suggest a counteroffer and you should repeat to them the advice you gave them at the time of original listing or in subsequent conversations with them when you reviewed the listed price, FMV and the market reaction from other showings.

Remember one important concept of your relationship with all your clients, whether you're representing both sides or just one: When you recognize the need for establishing a strong rapport with your clients, that special emotional and chemical process that takes place when you take the time to build that foundation of understanding wants and needs, you will have the ammunition and insight to represent them, in any situation. If you add to this rapport your own elements of loyalty, honesty, truthfulness and openness, you will have no difficulty whatever in representing both the buyer and seller and meeting both their needs.

CHAPTER

12 Building Referral Business

Your goal has been to develop long-lasting relationships with your satisfied clients, resulting from your superior performance in meeting their needs and continuing on into future business dealings with them and their friends because they trust you.

This entire manual has been instructing you in all aspects of real estate sales techniques and your own personal attitude toward them. We have discussed how to perform the skills, as well as the importance of the proper mental attitude required of you in order to perform them well. It brings to mind the story of Francis, a good old mule.

Through the years, Francis had been faithful in helping an old farmer. One morning, the farmer awoke at 3:00 A.M. and wasn't able to get back to sleep because he was thinking about old Francis. He finally got out of bed, put on his clothes and went out to the barn where Francis was in his stall. The farmer said, "Francis, old friend, tomorrow I am going to turn you out to the pasture; you're going to retire. All you'll have to do is eat and sleep from now on." Then the farmer, feeling redeemed, went back to bed.

The following day, as the sun rose, the farmer got up, dressed and took old Francis out to the pasture. There he removed the halter, slapped the mule on the side and turned him loose to graze. Over the next few days, the farmer saw Francis from time to time. Suddenly, however, he discovered the mule was missing.

The farmer searched the pasture, but old Francis was nowhere to be found. It occurred to the farmer that he hadn't looked down the old abandoned well, which had become overgrown with grass and weeds.

He immediately went there, and sure enough, there was old Francis standing down in the bottom of the well, switching his tail back and forth. The farmer was presented with quite a problem. He didn't want the mule to starve to death in the bottom of the well, and yet he didn't know how to get him out. After much thought, the farmer decided to get a shovel and began shoveling dirt into the well to bury old Francis right there. Each shovelful would land on the mule's back, but instead of just standing there, the mule would shake it off, step up, and stand on it. Shovelful after shovelful and the same thing occurred. Francis would shake the dirt off, step up, and stand on it. A few hours later, the dirt pile approached the top of the well and old Francis just stepped out and went down the pasture continuing to graze.

Fear, worry, failure and difficulty come to all of us. We, too, sometimes find ourselves in the so called "well of depression," but we have a choice. We can stand still, be overwhelmed and do nothing about it, or we can shake it off, and rise above it. We have that choice.

EARN LOYALTY FROM CUSTOMERS

Selling real estate is not just one transaction. It is not getting a listing and trying to sell it; it is not finding a buyer and selling him or her a home. It doesn't end there.

This is a personal business. Your success is based on many skills to perform, and a great deal of knowledge to accumulate, but your success is no greater than your ability to establish positive relationships with your clients.

The initial few hours you spend with customers are the most important, because they have to believe everything you tell them.

You are the specialist; you must earn their trust. How you conduct yourself, your honesty and openness, will instill in them that trust all the more as time goes by in your dealings with them. The customer will appreciate you, rather than take you for granted.

That last statement reminds me of a man and his wife who lived in a small home on the east side of a very big lake.

> Every morning, they would arise at sunup and begin work in their garden before the heat of the day. As they worked, they would gaze across the lake and see what appeared to be a castle. They knew it had to be a castle, because of the way the windows shone with a beautiful golden color.
>
> One day, the man was determined to take his boat and row across the lake to view the castle. It was noon before he arrived on the other side of the lake. He tied his boat to a small bush and walked the path to the castle on the hilltop. He found himself right in front of the anticipated castle, only to find that it was a small cottage, even more humble than his own. Frustrated and disappointed, he proceeded back to his boat and began rowing to his home where he would tell his wife about his experience. He rowed several hours and found himself still out in the lake at sundown. He looked toward his home and was amazed to see that it was now the one with the golden windows. Then he realized that for all these years, he had been living with an illusion.

This is so true of life. So often we see a false picture when we look at other people and their accomplishments. Don't overlook the gold in your windows, the precious little things that you might take for granted.

Buyers are only loyal when loyalty is earned. Behind every successful salesperson is a substantial referral business. A certain amount of referral business is a result of the conditions we mentioned before. However, the salespeople who earn substantial incomes from referrals have an organized plan for building a referral clientele as well.

REFERRAL-BUILDING PLANS

Clients You Have Represented

Action Step 1 Upon opening a transaction, record the following information on a 3" × 5" card or in your computer database: names of the entire family, any personal information relating to hobbies, interests, etc. On the back of the card, staple a copy of the listing of the property involved. Indicate final sales price and terms. File these cards alphabetically.

Action Step 2   If the client is employed by a company that will be transferring or hiring people, file the client's business card alphabetically by company name.

Action Step 3   Send a thank-you note prior to the closing, thanking your clients for their business and congratulating them on the transaction.

Action Step 4   After the transaction is closed, personally deliver a small gift to the clients, such as an indoor plant, an engraved name plate for the door or table decoration. It is not necessary to spend a great deal of money; this is just a remembrance.

Action Step 5   At least once a year, pay a personal visit to say hello. Always remember to refer to the children by name.

Action Step 6   Send a minimum of one card a year. Most salespeople prefer Christmas cards; however, birthday cards are excellent and are not as likely to be lost in the seasonal avalanche.

Corporate Clients

The keys to continual referrals from a company are the rapid and pleasant service to the employee and follow-up with the employer.

Action Step 1   Upon receiving the referral, contact the employee immediately and arrange an appointment.

Action Step 2   During the employee's move, send weekly progress reports to the company's referring executive.

Action Step 3   Immediately notify the company when the transactions are completed with their employees.

Action Step 4   Send a thank-you note to the executive who referred the employee.

Action Step 5 Most companies have a person who is responsible for incoming and outgoing employees. Maintain continual but low-profile contact through, for example, an occasional social lunch.

Religious or Charitable Organizations

Many salespeople are active in religious and charitable organizations. Quite often, these organizations are asked for recommendations about real estate. While some agents hesitate to pursue this business, it has many benefits to all parties:

- The organization benefits from additional income.
- The member feels more at ease with someone who is affiliated with the same organization.
- The salesperson gains additional income.

Action Step 1 Contact the person in charge.

Action Step 2 Offer to donate 10 percent of whatever income you receive from the transaction to the organization. *Note:* Most third-party referrals are 20 percent and, of course, your 10 percent charitable donation is tax-deductible.

Action Step 3 Follow up on referrals promptly and send a progress report to the referring person. The 10 percent donation should come directly from you, not your company.

Referrals Related to the Real Estate Industry

Many businesses have constant contact with potential buyers and sellers of real estate. Here is a partial list for your consideration:

- *Builders.* Buyers for their homes may have homes to list and sell.
- *Lenders.* These companies have properties taken in foreclosure.
- *Third-party companies.* Examples of these businesses include Ticor, Executrans, Home Equity and Merrill Lynch Relocation.

ACTION COMMITMENTS

I have read the previous section and realize I must do the following:

TO DO	TARGET DATE OF COMPLETION	ACTION COMPLETED
1.		
2.		
3.		
4.		
5.		
6. Meet with sales manager.		

Epilogue

DON'T STOP . . . GO TO THE TOP

I have spent my adult years fascinated by, and in search of, the answer to why people succeed in their chosen areas of endeavor. See if you can identify some people you know in the following story.

A group of athletes met in an inn at the foot of the majestic Swiss Alps to hear a famous mountain climber speak about his experiences. As his talk continued, many of the athletes became very enthusiastic about mountain climbing. After the talk was over, they approached the speaker and asked if he would guide them the following day on their own climb. He consented, so the following day they gathered all their gear and supplies together to start climbing the mountain.

They climbed for several hours, and finally arrived at a cabin halfway up the side of the mountain. This was a place to stop, relax, get warm and refresh themselves before they continued their ascent to the top. A fire was built, a pot of coffee was brewed and they all settled back for a short time. Soon, one of the climbers spoke to the guide and informed him that his ankle was bothering him from an old injury and that he was going to stay put and rejoin them on their descent.

Soon, another climber who had a sore foot asked if he could be excused, and said that he, too, would join the party again upon descent. One after one, others gave one excuse or another until there were just a few remaining to go to the top of the mountain. The rest remained at the cabin. In a short time, the remaining few climbers began the rest of the climb to the top.

About midday, one of the men who had remained at the cabin who was looking out the window toward the top of the mountain shouted, "Hey, look! There's Bob. . . Fred. . . there's the rest of them. They're going all the way to the top. They've made it to the top! "

This is the way it is with so many people. So many of us in life make a good start, but the going gets a little tough, and then we stop half-way. Often, we're not willing to keep climbing; we're not willing to pay the price for success. We'd rather make up some feeble excuse that sounds good and remain at the halfway mark while our peers go on to the top.

Remember, *success* begins with the same letter as *sacrifice*. Consider the following example:

There was a young musician who played in one of the finest symphony orchestras in Europe. Times were rough, and jobs were extremely difficult to find. Having a job with an orchestra was fantastic.

This young musician was on his way to developing his craft when he was struck with tragedy: He was losing his sight! He was afraid someone would find out and he would lose his job. So, secretly, he began to memorize the music at home, note by note. Soon, he began memorizing the other orchestra members' music, and after a while, he not only knew his music by heart, but every orchestra member's part as well.

He became an outstanding member of the orchestra, guarding closely his eyesight secret. He had prepared himself for the future when he wouldn't be able to see.

One night, the conductor became ill, and the young man was asked to conduct the orchestra. He approached the podium, took hold of the baton, closed the orchestra leader's score, and began to conduct the great symphony orchestra without ever referring to a single written note.

He had become a success because he was willing to pay the price for success. He went on to become one of the most noted conductors of symphonies throughout the world; his name? Arturo Toscanini.

Success can be achieved in everything from parenting to gardening, music, finances, sports, even the presidency of the United States. In each case, these individuals had a dream or goal, the courage to get started persist and the self-discipline not to quit.

On the face of it, it seems absurdly simple, doesn't it? Finding a dream or goal, that's easy. Get started. We usually handle that, although overcoming inertia sometimes does take effort. But now we separate the wheat from the chaff. It's easy and fun to get started on something. Excitement and enthusiasm are running high, the band is playing, the crowd is yelling, it's the thrill of the new adventure.

After those things have faded into the distance, you're left out there, alone, with no cheering and night falling. It seems you're the only one left with that dream. You're tired, dirty, sweaty and you're still a long way from completion. You start to question, if this is so much fun, why am I the only one left out there, still flailing away at it? Maybe everyone else knows something you don't. Maybe it can't be done, or if it can, it's not worth the effort. These thoughts start entering your mind. As your physical and mental energy slackens, you start to get some serious doubts, and maybe even grind to a halt.

But it's right here at this point, where you are poised to achieve success, that you decide: Despite all odds, you're going to keep at it! for the next three hours, four days, five months or even six years. With this decision, you're on your way!

Decide now what you want from life before it's too late. One last story to remember on your road to success:

A little boy went to an wise old man in his town, and said, "I'm told you can give me the secret of happiness and success in life. Please sir, I want to know that secret."

After a moment, the wise old man stood up, took the little boy's hand and led the boy down the path to the lake. He didn't stop at the lake's edge; instead they continued right into the water.

The water was soon up to the lad's knees, then his chest and finally over his head. The old wise man held the boy's head under the water for five seconds, 10 seconds, 15 and then turned and led the boy out of the water, back to dry land and safety.

Upon the edge of the water, the wise old man said, "Son, what did you want more than anything else in the world when you were under the water?"

The little boy answered quickly, "A breath of air." The wise old man said, "Son, when you are determined to find success in life as badly as you wanted a breath of air, you will have found the secret to success and happiness."

This process is certainly no great discovery or breakthrough on my part. It's no well-guarded secret of millionaires or high achievers.

It is nature's way that we have dreams and ambitions that excite us into ACTION. And it is also nature's way to provide us with a constitution that can achieve whatever is needed to complete those dreams and ambitions. So don't abort your mission, don't quit; because each morning brings us so many wonderful days ahead in our life, endowed with all that's necessary to reach our goals and our dreams.

Remember, today is the first day of the rest of your life, so make the most of it!

Index